ABC's for Seniors

Large
Print

ABC's *for* seniors

Successful Aging Wisdom
from an Outrageous Gerontologist

RUTH HARRIET JACOBS, Ph.D.
ILLUSTRATIONS BY DYLAN SMITH

Hatala Geroproducts • Greentop, Missouri

Published in the United States of America by
Hatala Geroproducts
Greentop, MO 63546 (population: 427)
09 08 07 06 05   1 2 3 4 5

ABC's for Seniors: Successful Aging Wisdom
from an Outrageous Gerontologist
by Ruth Harriet Jacobs

ISBN-10: 1-933167-44-0
ISBN-13: 978-1-933167-44-2
LC control number: 2006924185

Some verses appeared in *Senior Times*, an award-winning newspaper in which the author has a monthly column, "Dr. Ruth Reports." They are used with the permission of *Senior Times*. All other verses were written for this book.

Cover and title page: Shaun Hoffeditz
Interior illustrations: Dylan Smith
Composition: Paula Presley Editorial Services
Body type: Adobe Tiepolo Book 15/18
Display type: P22 Victorian Swash

Contents

Part 1 ✳ Alphabet

A is for aging. 3
B is for bolder 5
C is for congratulations 7
C is for councils on aging 10
D is for depression. 12
D is for depression. 15
E is for education 17
F is for fun 21
G is for gerontology and geriatrics. 23
H is for heat and hypothermia. 25
I is for I 28
J is for join 31
K is for key 32
L is for love. 35
M is for memory. 37
M is for memoir 40
N is for nature 42
O is for odd 44
P is for pack rat. 46
P is for pets. 49
Q is for question 50
R is for rage. 52
S is for spots. 54
T is for tomato 57
U is for useful tips 59
V is for volunteer. 63
W is for walk and water 65
X is for Xerox 67
Y is for youth 69
Z is for zealot 71
Alphabet in one poem 72

Part 2 ✳ Prose Advice

Forgive Yourself First 77

Crimes I Have Committed Often 80

You Do Deserve Sunshine In Your Life 81

It's Time To Get Familiar With the RASP's Nest 82

Reverse Birthday Gifts 88

It's *Your* Brain—Use It or Lose It 93

People-Watching 97

Limit Yourself To One Yard Sale Each Weekend . . . 102

Fearing Retirement? 106

Humor 111

Safe Driving Renewal 115

Of Course We Are "Weirder" 119

The Ups and Downs of Aging Courageously 123

Exploring 128

Mother-in-Law/Daughter-in-Law Relationships . . . 132

Reflections From the '70s 137

Journaling 143

Some Resolutions for Older People 147

Illness 150

An Open Letter to Doctors 155

Antideterioration and Sleep Suggestions 159

New Things To Do 164

Bereavement, Loneliness, and the Holidays 169

Beating Summer Heat 174

Changing Rules 178

Moving Your Home 183

Friends 189

Good Accumulating 192

Ten Areas Where We Can Choose 194

A Variety of Suggestions for Older People 196

Possible Activities for Older People 199

About the Author 200

Part 1
Alphabet

A is for aging

A is for aging that is not enraging,
as seasoned citizens continue sageing,
empowered by verses of Mother Ruth
in alphabet form like Mother Goose.
This alphabet of gerontology
will teach how to avoid melancholy
so you can celebrate your later years
with cheers, and birthdays without tears
or downing excess gin and beers.

Author Mother Ruth is also Doctor Ruth,
who knows gerontology's truth,
gleaned from solid deep research
plus her seventy-eight-year-old perch.
If you follow Mother Ruth's advice
your aging will be very nice;
you will become courageous,
wise, witty, and maybe outrageous.
It can be fun to turn the page
from naïve youth to aging sage.

Read onward now from A through Z
to see what good old age can be.
At the end there is no quiz,
but you will be an aging whiz.

B is for bolder

B is for bolder
when you get older.
Do what you want to do
let nobody step on you.
Don't do what you're told
ignore messages sold.

Be forceful and brave,
get out of your cave,
ride on a wave.
Being old, you're bright,
and have second sight.

If not now, when?
Speak up again and again
tell kids, women, and men
what is true and right.
Use senior might,
fly a bright kite,
see every sight,
dance every night,
enjoy the moonlight,
eat a tempting bite,
climb every height,
even with cane
or arthritic pain.

You're a survivor
and a great thriver.
File shyness in a folder
be warmer, not colder.

C is for congratulations

C is for hearty congratulations.
From genes or health machinations
you have reached the high years
envied by young dears.

Dying young is a shame;
being old gives claim
to rich retirement years
with leisure, fun, and cheers.

You've climbed life rung by rung
know more than the young.
Know what is minor,
what is medium, or finer.
You shouldn't waste time
squeezing a dime
or buying useless stuff
of which you have enough.

The ads in our mail
that promise a bale,
seem too good to be true,
are really goose poo.

Hang up on salespeople
who think the old are feeble.

Don't fall for any sales scam
for things not worth a damn.

We don't want to trip on rugs
or collect dust, mice, or bugs,
so we simplify our quarters,
dump furniture on daughters,
unload our junk on others—
nieces, nephews, young mothers.
Garage sales are our specialty;
who needs a hundred cups for tea?

9 «

C is for councils on aging

I love Councils on Aging
and find it very "en-caging"
when seniors stay home alone
instead of picking up the phone
to discover what is going on
and finding a new dawn
with friendly peers
enjoying their later years.

Here's to the wonderful Councils on Aging
despite low budgets and salaries enraging
they reach out to elders who are frail
and active seniors by newspaper and mail
with help, advice, programs, and trips,
and welcoming smiles on their lips.

Here's to great drop-in and senior centers
full of fun, education, and good mentors.
Here's to nourishing, friendly lunches
and other treats for seasoned citizen munchers.

C.O.A. directors, boards, and workers, I love you
for all the daily unsung good you always do.
For advocating so well for the aging cause
give yourselves a hearty round of applause.

D is for depression

D is for depression, the dumps.
Sometimes elders go into slumps.
Men usually try to tough it out
when they should give a shout
to physicians and others who aid
even though they must be paid.

When depression is durable,
get help because it's curable.
Therapy can uncover causes
let us deal with aging losses
and change our sad lifestyle
so we can be happy in a while.

Getting help doesn't mean you're crazy
not getting it may make you hazy, lazy
drooping around the house night and day
when with help there is a better way.

Make sure you get a thorough check up
ruling out things that wreck up
your mood, such as poor nutrition,
low thyroid, or other medical condition.
Our aging bodies are prone to woes,
but medicine can keep us on our toes.

Certain medicines may be villains, too,
and can be changed when doctor sees you.

Being depressed is no disgrace;
it happens to the human race.
You are not the only sad case;
get help, change your pace.

You can get referrals by paging
your doctor or services for aging,
so don't just sit there blue
when there are ways to help you.

D is for depression

—for doctors and others who care for elders

Is depression repression,
being censored aggression,
or is it expression
of old age despair,
or need for body repair
and better self care?
Is it from drinking
or negative thinking
about early life dramas
and current traumas?

Is it from illness and meds
that elders take to their beds?
If confusion makes them look crazy
are they demented or merely hazy?

Depression appears like dementia
if depression provides self-censure;
results in poor sleep and grooming
and obsessing about threats looming.

Depression can be near
if an elder can't hear
or vision's not clear

or grief is for one dear
and other stresses and losses—
even retirement forced by bosses,
and lack of caring, handy folks
to provide positive strokes.

There are more questions must be posed
if depression is diagnosed
and appropriate treatment proposed.

Writing off depression as part of age
means the professional is not sage,
because depression is beatable
being eighty percent treatable.
Elders can be helped with coping,
and return to energy and hoping.

E is for education

E is for education,
no longer for vocation,
but for stimulation
to keep brain cells glowing
and prevent us from slowing.

Early we had some schooling
now it's time for retooling
to learn what is new
will enrich, exult you.

So shine your glasses;
take adult ed classes
in your city or town
or go for cap and gown
as prices aren't high
at colleges nearby
seniors go free
or for minor fee.

Don't fear a school bell,
as elders learn well.
You have will and skill
aren't over the hill.

Elder hostels everywhere
have faculty who care.

The catalog is there
11 Ave. De Lafayette, Boston, MA, 02111
Get it and be ready to go
for a week's study and recreation,
a terrific learning vacation
at colleges and conference centers
where you'll meet mentors.

Senior Venture has classes and more
in western states you will adore;
for catalog call 1-800-257-0577
and soon you'll be in heaven.

Elderhostel and Interhostel for an added sum
have intergenerational programs where
                  children come
Interhostel of NH arranges these,
along with trips and cruises that please;
phone 603-862-1147

Or study on your own
with books your library can loan
dendrites in your brain will grow
the more you learn and know.

F is for fun

F is for fun—
do have a ton
alone or with a mate
you should celebrate.

It's time to take Fun 101
now your hard work is done.
All your lifelong
you knew right from wrong
and worked hard in house
or for a boss, the louse,
so now it's time to do
what amuses you.

Give someone a ring-o
to go to bingo
or whatever pleasure
gives you treasure
you can measure
by joy and laughter
that lingers after.

Fun is no perversion;
go on an excursion,
tell and play jokes
with good sport folks

read what's not serious,
including the mysterious.

It really is dandy
if children are handy.
You provide the fun
while their parents run.
Take a child to the zoo,
and you'll enjoy it too.

Old age isn't for dulls;
whatever turns you on, indulge.

G is for gerontology and geriatrics

G is for gerontology
where experts in biology,
sociology, psychology,
economics, and physiology
study aging folks,
their functioning and hopes
in the context of society
with infinite variety.
Gerontologists at a college
teach and add to knowledge.

Geriatrics, on the other hand,
designates the medical band.
Scientists, nurses, and docs
are in the geriatric box,
helping with your health,
adding to their wealth.

Geriatric doctors are rare;
it's hard to get their care.
Geriatrics isn't highly paid
from Medicare or Medicaid,
so docs tend to specialties
which reimburse high fees.

H is for heat and hypothermia

H is for excess heat,
which we must beat;
also being older,
we can't risk colder.

When temperature soars
better to be indoors
with cooled air or fan.
In youth you maybe ran
but now heat prostration
can cause fatal dehydration.
Drink lots of water, rest,
don't flunk this test.
Macular degeneration harasses
so do wear sunglasses.
Another reason to stay in
is summer sun hurts old skin.
Wear a hat and sun screen
skin cancer can be mean.
Go outdoors early in the days
or late to minimize sun rays.

In winter, hypothermia kills
elders who get excessive chills
by keeping thermostats down
or walking too long in town.

Spend money on heat
tell others you meet.
If your heater goes
get shelter when it snows.

I is for I

I is for I, number one.
All your life, you've run,
doing for others
as mothers or brothers.
As workers or spouse,
you couldn't be a louse,
so you put others first,
and took the worst.
Sometimes you felt cursed,
in altruism rehearsed.
Now is time to be first.

Buy yourself a gift
to give you a lift.
Here is a tip.
Give yourself a trip.
Don't be dim,
indulge each whim.
Your time has come
your rights begun.

Make a list of things
that always brings
boredom or misery
and silently agree

you did that stuff
long enough.

Make another list
of things you missed
and start doing those.

It's time you chose.
I is not a dirty word
to put I last is absurd.

J is for join

J is for join, connect, and network,
or loneliness can lurk.
Your longtime friends are great,
yet never too many or too late—
enrich your life by adding more.
Improve your mental health score.

You need someone in whom to confide
things you usually suppress or hide.
You need crisis folks who'll help out
creating support networks is the route.

You need casual friends to play
bridge or sports or what way
you like to fill your time, which grows
when retirement means paid work goes.

Organizations, religious groups, and clubs
are healthier settings than pubs
in which to spend your time. Be involved
and your emotive, social needs are solved.

Some time alone is necessary, it's true,
but people affirm and stimulate you.
Check your local paper for meetings
go, extend your hand and greetings.

K is for key

K is for key
where can it be?
Then we have to look
for that checkbook.

So as not to be surprised
we have to be organized.
In later years we have to get
a routine so we'll be set.
Each item has to have a space
so we can find it in its place.

Hang keys by the door
so we won't have to roar.
Mine are chained to purse
so I won't have to curse.

My shopping list has a home;
otherwise, it would roam.
Keep boots by the door
be ready for downpour.

Since an overdose kills,
record you've downed pills
by checking off the date
on a calendar or slate.

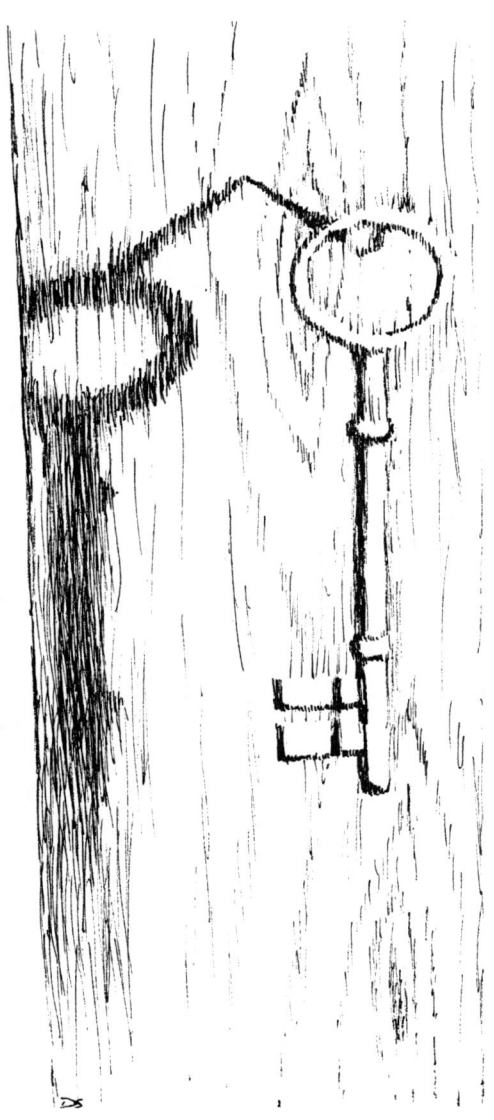

Also if you eliminate clutter
you'll not have to mutter,
and if you use more light
things will be easy to sight.

L is for love

L is for love, including sex,
sometimes ruined by medical treks
that prescribe drugs harming libido.
This is not the way to go.
Losing desire or erection
may plunge you into dejection.
Should that happen, don't be shy.
Speak up, ask your physician why
you can't take a different pill
that won't preclude sexual thrill.

Old age sex can be sweet,
unless you so fear defeat
that you won't even try,
and pass opportunity by,
having absorbed ageist jokes
that ridicule sex of older folks.

Don't believe ancient tales
that sex is over for old males.
Techniques are better today
so love can find a way.
Penile implants can aid
if prostate makes you betrayed.

Orgasms for women are there
long after gray hair;
vaginal lubricants may be needed,
and directions for positions heeded.

Coitus may take longer,
but pleasure can be stronger.
No danger he's too quick,
or she'll be morning sick!

Books and experts can aid;
well worth the money paid.

Just cuddling can be fine,
and massage, a pleasant time.
Those who do not have a mate
can self-stimulate.

M is for memory

M is for memory, good or bad,
which recalls the past we had.
For some, our chief complaint
is that our memory just ain't.
We forget phones and a name
our memory isn't the same.
Odd, we recall our kindergarten class,
but check to see if there's a wet glass
so we know we brushed teeth or took meds.
Forgetting makes us distrust our heads.

Some forgetting is normal; don't despair.
There are memory tricks to help repair.
AARP can rent or sell you a video cheap.[1]
"Memory: The Long and Short of It" is a leap
for remembering names and things,
and dealing with lapses aging brings.

Forgetting may be because you can't hear;
the initial message was unclear.
So get your hearing checked real quick
if you want what was said aloud to stick.

---

1 AARP's address is 601 E. Street NW, Washington, DC 20077-2400.

Long-term memory is better in old days
so reminiscing alone or to others pays.
Short-term memory may not be as great,
but don't assume Alzheimer's is your fate.

Your nutrition may have lacks,
or stress may be in heavy packs.
Depression may cause memory losses,
or oppression by nasty bosses.
A good check up can help us solve
why our memory seems to dissolve.

Enjoy the happy memories of your life;
let go those of pain and strife.
Living so long means
memories are there in reams and dreams
so if we forget something here and there
we really shouldn't worry or care.

M is for memoir

Write it out of love;
write it out of hate;
write it to find out
how you arrived here
and which path waits;
write it for your heirs,
yourself, or the world

Don't worry about sequences,
or try to do it all at once;
instead write as you recall
odors you can still inhale,
sounds you can still hear,
things you can still see,
food you can still taste,
textures you can still touch

Remember your grandparents,
remember your mother and
father, sisters, brothers;
remember the good teachers,
remember the bad teachers
remember your best friend,
and the bully you feared;
remember your first love,
first car, first employer,

children; write about these

Look at old family photos;
look at your school ones;
recall your feelings then,
describe them in words

Think about houses
where you've lived—
your beds, kitchens,
clothes in closets,
treasures, collections—
tell about them
and change-points
or epiphanies

When stuck, read other memoirs;
read mine, delight my publisher;
see how they are organized—
what are the themes;
find the theme in your life,
organize your gleanings,
celebrate, and share
your memoir.

N is for nature

N is for nature, which comforts and delights,
now that we have time to listen and see sights.
Lakes, rivers, flowers, birds, and trees,
all of these lovely gifts please
our senses. Beauty lowers our defenses
so we no longer brood, simmer, and curse
but we feel in tune with the universe.

Seasoned citizens get Golden Eagle passes
for National Parks where nature masses,
or they can visit a local nature preserve.
At our ages, we certainly deserve.

Feeding birds or ducks is pure pleasure;
on bird walks you can spot a treasure.
Mountain majesty viewing can make us gasp,
though climbing them is a task.

Looking at the stars with telescope or eye
makes us familiar with the nighttime sky.
Doing this we have a wonderful time
exploring an endless gold mine.

O is for odd

O is for being odd.
Get out of the P pod
of proper and prim;
stretch every limb;
be eccentrically you,
one of the few,
who doesn't conform,
who is newborn
in later years
to lead peers
courageously,
outrageously
model new roles
not rigid poles

What can they do
to punish you
if you renew,
wear every hue?

Get wild clothes,
wiggle your toes
in comfy shoes;
do what you choose.

Eschew quiet patterns,
wear silks and satins;
skip well bred,
wild hat on head.

Try new things—
wear flashy rings,
be one of the few
to take a new cue.

Don't be lazy;
be a little crazy!
What's at stake
is being AWAKE.

R is for pack rat

—Pathetic pack rat's plea

Please car, don't stop at garage sales.
I already have bales and bales
of garage sale stuff,
which leaving behind was tough,
because prices were cheap,
so my home already has a heap
of trash I shouldn't keep.

Please eyes, avert from a sidewalk
with good discards that talk—
like furniture which says "free"
that I'd better not see.

Please hands, don't grab a book,
no matter how good it may look;
ignore any cheap or used book sale,
or don't order books by mail,
as my bookcases overflow
with books on floor below
or books wherever I go,
piled high on every table
that I'll read them is a fable.

Please feet, don't have agility
at the town's disposal facility;
stay away from the take and leave;
if I say I'll leave, I deceive.

Please nose, don't smell out church fairs
with junk from other people's lairs;
their white elephants I don't need
and should go away with speed.

Please memory, forget I was a poor child;
it is long enough I've been wild
to seek out, collect, and keep;
my piles are much too deep.
Time to throw out, reform, retreat;
being clutter free would be sweet;
it would be nice to be neat,
but there's a garage sale down the street.

P is for pets

P is for pets,
who require vets,
and food, and care,
but they are there
with eyes that glisten
as they love and listen.

This gerontologist knows
aging research shows
after a heart attack
pet owners get health back,
dog owners must walk a pet
so their exercise is set.

Besides, we get delightful vibes
from pets instead of diatribes.
To pat a pet is pleasure;
their companionship a treasure.

Q is for question

Q is for question, again and again
whenever professional women and men
are giving you aging medical advice
because, frankly, some are not nice
about giving enough thought and time
seeing too many folks in an hour
and exercising too much power.
It is your mind, body, and life
and you don't need the strife
of a doctor who doesn't care
or acts as if you're not there.
I am saying, watch out, beware.
Ageism infects professionals as well.
If it does, give them restrained hell.
Let them think you are worthy indeed
that you think, you read, you bleed.

Take a list of meds you already take
so a doctor will not make a mistake
of giving you something that will combine
to give your organs a really bad time.

If you have side effects from a med
don't think it's just in your head.
Call the doctor and ask for a review
this could be life saving for you.

If your doctor is a terrible pain
and you've tried again and again
to get better service, check out
a better one; get rid of the lout.

R is for rage

R is for rage
common at any age
when people hurt us
or events make us fuss.

Holding rage in
is a serious sin;
inward turned mad
means you are sad.

Better to fight
than be polite
if you are hurt
or folks are curt.

Don't be in a cage
of righteous rage.
Speak out
give a shout.

Don't hit or shoot,
that won't suit;
but express pain
in verbal refrain.

Avoid bad results
of swallowing insults
by defending you.
You're human, too!

S is for spots

S is for spots
of which we get lots
if our hand is unsteady
or our mouth unready.
Soups, sauces can burst
off our spoon, but the worst
is tomato covered pasta—
will that come out, I ask ya?

Thankfully, as we spot more
20/20 vision is out the door;
we don't see those messy dots,
are blissfully unaware of spots.

However, we must check our garments
not to be labeled sloppy by varmints
always ready to criticize those older
in tones meaner and colder.

We can outwit critical folk
even if we can't remove with soap
little mementos of our meals.
In triumph we kick up our heels
by pinning on great slogan buttons
that hide we were gluttons.

We can wear hilarious pins
or buttons of a candidate who wins.
We can proudly proclaim our pain
over political issues and gain
favorable attention from words
that salute whatever scarce birds
or whales in which we invest
by putting buttons on over dirty vest.

Scarves are also a dashing ploy
that may look festive or coy,
but are really hiding coffee
that won't wash out for me.

We aged are clever;
given challenge, we endeavor
to surmount. So "out dread spot"
we say, using strategies we've got.

T is for tomato

T is for tomato (and broccoli, carrot, fruit).
If you want to fit in dress, jeans, or suit
you need to eat veggies. Good nutrition
will help you age in excellent condition.

We need diets low in fat
with proteins that
are in grains, beans, and such.
With salt, we need a light touch.

Sugar should be limited too, boo-hoo
and caffeine is not good for you.
But vegetables and fruits are ideal
for snacks or to fill out a meal.

Calcium is in low fat or skim milk,
leafy greens, and stuff of that ilk.
Reading labels is an acquired art
for those of us who wish to part
with high fat, high sodium stuff
and get vitamins enough.

If you are alone or cooking is hard,
Twinkies, toast, and jam disgard.
Sign up for a well-balanced lunch
with a senior center bunch.

Don't be proud or self neglect.
There are services you can select.
Meals On Wheels will do the trick
should you get sick.

U is for useful tips

USEFUL TIP 1:
If married a decade
divorced people can be paid
at social security age
50 per cent of ex-spouse's "wage"
from social security money
with 100% still to former honey.
Then, if ex-spouse dies
the 50 percent multiplies
so survivor gets 100 percent
which helps pay rent.
If half is less than own S.S.
you can first say "Yes,
I'll collect on my own until
he goes under graveyard hill;
then if his 100 percent is more than mine,
for his S.S. I'll quickly sign."

USEFUL TIP 2:
Ask wherever you go
be quick, not shy, or slow.
Request senior discounts
so saving mounts.

USEFUL TIP 3:
Another cue I can give

is to consider where to live.
Should you stay in a big home
which makes it hard to roam
because heat may fail
or no one takes in mail?
Could you rent a room or two
to someone who could do
chores while you're away, or play
and be there to say "good day"?
Or should you simplify your life
in a retirement place without strife
because meals and events are there
and perhaps also health care?
But beware, check out finances
don't take foolish chances
hustlers are everywhere
they don't care.

USEFUL TIP 4:
Indoor swimming pools
often include in their rules
cheap rates for senior swimmers.
Such exercise makes winners.

USEFUL TIP 5:
Seasoned citizens have looked around
and smartly found
needs in their areas unmet
and offered services that get
income, activity, and meaning,

and prevent boredom screaming.
Seniors care for absent folks' pets
sell handicrafts, food, and onion sets.

USEFUL TIP 6:
In old age we don't sleep as long;
panicking about this is wrong.
It is not sleeping pills you need
watch early A.M. or late TV or read.

USEFUL TIP 7:
Scatter rugs and electric cords,
clutter, slippery floor boards
cause falls with broken bones
that bring hospitals and moans.
So elder-proof house for self
and don't climb up high shelf.
Don't save by cutting bulb watts.
Turn off gas under your pots.
Use a timer to remind food is done.
Accidents are no fun!

USEFUL TIP 8:
Some people believe elders can't think
which drives you to the brink of drink.
Speak up for yourself and old others;
all ages are sisters and brothers.

V is for volunteer

V is for volunteer
helping child, midlifer, or peer
or working for a worthy cause
to aid society or alter laws.

You have the skills and tools
to help hospitals and schools.
Lots of other local groups
can use old age troops.

Agencies can help you find
a placement where your mind
will grow with stimulation
while you help the nation.

In addition, you can be
a volunteer for AARP
Write Volunteer Talent Bank,
601 E. Street N.W., Washington, DC., 20077-2400

Volunteers often get pay,
and volunteering is a way
more meaningful than play
to spend an hour or a day.

Volunteers have looked outward
and seen life is hard,
for some are marred
by tragedy and jarred
by crises and society's discard.

A volunteer has a good heart
and is very smart
whether pushing a book cart
serving fruit or a tart,
or addressing a part
of a problem to help start
the healing art.

Volunteers are people who
respond to troubles' cue,
volunteering to do
work of love so true,
kind through and through.
Volunteers I salute you.

W is for walk and water

W is for walk.
Don't just talk
about getting in shape;
throw on coat or cape.
Outdoors is the place to go,
even if you start slow.

Do five minutes to start.
Walking is good for your heart.
Add more minutes each day
and you'll be on your way.

If the weather is bad
and you're mad or sad
go walk in a mall
with a friend you call,
or walk alone and stare
at interesting people there.

But don't walk into a shop
for a sundae with hot fudge on top.

W is also for water
remember you oughta
drink eight glasses a day
to keep illness away.

X is for Xerox

X is for Xerox®, a terrific way
to circulate what you have to say.
Now is the time to write your memoir,

telling descendents what came before
they and even you and others arrived.
Tell how the family derived
on all four grandparents' streams.
Certainly, you could write reams.

Or Xerox your political wisdom and view
and send it out to publications, too.
Letters to the editor relieve your stress
at the nonsense politicians profess.

Xerox a wonderful, newsy December letter
no bought card could please friends better.
Think of the money you can save
in addition to hearing recipients rave.

Write some poems and Xerox them, too;
it could open a new career for you.
Or Xerox petitions to improve your city;
being a passive citizen is a pity.

Xerox cartoons for your friends and kin;
making folks laugh is definitely in.
Xerox your favorite recipes and share
with others, including a newlywed pair.

Xerox when filing taxes or Medicare papers;
the mail sometimes does mysterious capers.
Better to have copies to prove you sent
such things as utilities checks and the rent.

Y is for youth

Y is for youth,
to tell the truth;
a turbulent time,
no reason or rhyme;
seeking identity,
very little serenity.

Don't be uncouth
mourning your youth;
copying young ways
hardly ever pays.
You'll look a silly
Mary Anne or Billy.

Don't envy young folk
or jealously poke
at their new ways
if you want praise.
Y is for your today
best act in the play.

You know who you are,
having come far;
your identity is clear

at last, you're a seer.
You have a long view;
no youth smart as you.

Z is for zealot

Z is for zealot
someone who will tell it
and re-tell it again
with word or pen.

A zealot for happy aging,
Mother Ruth's been paging
you by alphabet verse,
wanting better, not worse.

She hopes you are zealous, too,
doing what is best for you.
So spread the word—
choosing misery is absurd.

Better to age the best we can
meeting later years with élan.
Be proud
not cowed.
Instead of raging,
ENJOY Your Aging.

Alphabet in one poem

—An overview alphabet for aging well

A is for ACTIVITY
better than passivity.
B is for BRAVERY
with some comic knavery.
C is for CARING.
D is for DARING.
E is for ERRING.

F is for FORGIVING
others and yourself,
FREELY living.
G is for GIVING
but also GETTING.
H is for HEALTH
and for HELPING
by volunteering.
I is for INSPIRATION
believing God helps.

J is for JOKES and fun.
K is for KNOWLEDGE, of which
we have a ton.
L is for LOVE in old age.
M is for MATRIARCHS, very sage.

N is for NATURE profound
and beauty to enjoy all around.

O is for OPPORTUNITY
to attend the university
in our later years
with young people and age peers.
P is for wise PATRIARCHS
old men who get good marks.
Q is for QUESTS and QUESTIONING
that makes our brains sing.
R is for REMINISCENCE
remembering our life's dance.
S is for SEXUALITY
which is not banality.
T is for THEATER and TRAVEL
and TRUTHS still to unravel.

U is for UNDERSTANDING
long life has given us.
V is for VARIETY and VITALITY.
W is for WISE WORDS
X is for XEROXING
to send those words
like birds flying.

Y is for YOU, survivor seers,
greeting your later years
With Z for ZEST
with cheers, not tears
or fears, my dears.
Our alphabet is done.
Your challenge has begun.

Part 2

Prose Advice

Readers, our alphabet is done, and now there is still more advice Dr. Ruth has to give about aging well and I offer it to you in prose form. Some of these suggestions and comments appeared in my monthly column "Dr. Ruth Reports" in the award-winning *Senior Times* distributed throughout New England. They are reprinted here with the permission of the publisher, Jane Jackson.

Forgive Yourself First

To forgive others is easier than forgiving oneself. Some people continue through life feeling guilty about certain thoughts or acts. Your Dr. Ruth has encountered many people of age, mostly women, who beat up on themselves unmercifully. They would never blame others for things that they feel were their own transgressions.

Women berate themselves for mistakes made with their children long after the children are grown. The truth is, these women did the best they could at the time considering the circumstances of their own lives and the state of society. They forgot there are few perfect parents who never made a mistake.

Whatever goes wrong with their children through life, they blame themselves. They forget that their progeny have minds of their own and there were other influences in the lives of children like schools, mass media, fathers, peers, et cetera.

They apologize to descendents for mistakes. Since parent-blaming is epidemic in America, the descendents are all too ready to concur that damage was done.

Both women and men blame themselves for financial mistakes, forgetting or choosing to deny that crystal balls were not available and that even top economists and financial experts make mistakes and lose money too.

Some religions tend to immerse people in guilt, but I do not think this is the entire explanation. I surmise that many feel a loss of power as they age. After retirement from work and parenting they may feel less important and of lower status. This eats at them and they reminisce about periods in life when they had more of an authority status. They begin to brood about whether or not they used power wisely or benignly. Instead of putting on rose colored glasses, they don dark ones. Mourning loss of power transforms in a peculiar way to feeling their power was dangerous or misguided.

Certainly, not all elders do this. Some take joy in recalling their accomplishments in the domestic, work, and other spheres. They focus on what they did well and forget alleged failures or mistakes. However, some brooders seek consolation or absolution from therapists or clergy. One New Age therapist suggests people write their so-called mistakes or sins on pieces of paper and have a ritual burning of them or some other way of ceremoniously letting them go. "Pour bleach on them" she suggests.

Some people try to wipe out what they consider their past bad deeds by doing good deeds. They give money they can't afford to descendents or charity. They do favors for everyone in sight hoping to rack up gold stars and self-esteem. I have seen people exhaust themselves in an endeavor to prove (to themselves) that they are good, worthy, and wonderful. This is precisely because they feel so bad about themselves.

This dance of retribution is sad. Sometimes it works but for the most part it becomes addictive or dysfunctional and usually misdirected. Beneficiaries of largesse are not always grateful. Rather, some resent being thought incapable and in need of help.

I know this because I have often tried excessively to help others to prove how good I am. I confess this as I too find myself brooding about past misdemeanors. We all long to be saints, not sinners.

I still brood about refusing to give money to a beggar at age eighteen when I was working full-time at a job that barely supported me. Sixty years later, I can still see the face of that beggar. I recently mentioned this in a group of friends and a wise friend said, "Let go of it." Maybe we need to confess our guilts publicly to diminish their hold on us. With this in mind, I share with my friendly readers, the following conversation in verse form.

Crimes I Have Committed Often

I have inflated students' grades
at various colleges where I've taught.
I have sampled from grocery bins
that say Do Not Sample
and swiped extra plastic bags
from supermarkets for trash.
I've sprayed myself with pricey perfume
from bottles in boutiques,
and rubbed their lotion
into my greedy hands

Once when I ran out of toilet paper
I stole a roll from the college
so I wouldn't have to stop
to get some on the way home.
I've taken handfuls of paper clips
from the self-serve copy center,
and I've forgotten to pay for coffee
drunk while pushing my shopping cart.

I've written glowing references
for somewhat incompetent friends,
and told many other lies
to help needy people.
I've put more sheets in an envelope
than one stamp will cover
figuring it will get delivered anyway,
which it usually does.

I've told numerous parents
    that their children are bright and beautiful
    when the kids were ugly and rather stupid.
    I've given second-hand books as gifts
    and let receivers think they were new.

Readers might find it useful also to confess their errors and then forgive themselves as they would forgive others. I love to do acrostics. I hope you enjoy this one about forgiveness.

You Do Deserve Sunshine In Your Life

Forgive yourself
Otherwise you might get depressed,
Rehashing unwise choices,
Grading yourself badly,
Instead of realizing
Very few people
Evaded mistakes.
Nobody is perfect.
Even you or me
Slip sometimes.
Stop punishing yourself.

It's Time To Get Familiar With the RASP's Nest

Here I present a short story that though fictitious represents characters and a place that is true to life. The story is intended to suggest means of advocacy for seasoned citizens, to empower them.

When Sam O. Brown, director of Pleasant Valley Retirement Complex, posted the residents' new rules received from corporate headquarters, he underestimated Sara and her cronies.

At 80, Sara, a gadabout to senior citizen free courses, got frustrated with ice and snow because she could no longer shovel her stairs and driveway and she got tired of her children worrying about her living alone. Her son and daughter pointed out that Pleasant Valley would return 90 percent of her pay-in if she was unhappy there and she knew also that 90 percent would go to her kids if she died. It seemed reasonable to swap her high maintenance house for a spotless apartment, services, companionship, and organized activities.

One of the first residents, Sara turned herself into an unofficial welcoming committee as others moved in. The food was adequate at the three meals provided although she noticed it was at its best when potential residents and their children came for a sample meal. She also enjoyed the recreational evenings and health and education lectures, frequent during the marketing period. She loved swimming in the indoor pool, which she often had to herself. She hoped the library would eventually house something besides Readers' Digest condensed books and old AARP magazines, but she still drove in daylight so she went to the town library for books and gave rides or got books for other residents.

She met people by hanging out in the front lobby with its ostentatious chandelier, and she found the easy chairs great for observing comings and goings. Sometimes she fell asleep there. At meals she sat with different people to size them up and hear their stories.

Gradually the place got fuller. Sara went into shock when Sam O. Brown posted the new rules.

Rule number one was that since near capacity had been reached, there would be three sittings at meals and residents would be assigned to one of the three meal times: Breakfast at 7:00, lunch at 11:00, dinner at 4:00; or breakfast at 8:00, lunch at noon, dinner at 5:00; or breakfast at 9:00, lunch at 1:00, and dinner at 6:00. Also, people were assigned to a specific table to eat all three meals with the same three other people. Space precluded, said the rules, that anyone eat alone or with less than three people.

"Ridiculous to have to eat on schedule and with the same people all the time," Sara announced to everyone in earshot of the management.

Rule two was that residents could swim only when a lifeguard was on duty. The lifeguard would be there only Wednesdays from 10:00 to 12:00 and Sundays from 2:00 to 4:00 when grandchildren and other guests could also swim. "That means only one swim a week," Sara complained. "with a bunch of kids in the pool, I can't do laps on Sundays." She got nowhere with Sam O. Brown who she called by his convenient initials S.O.B.

Rule three was that residents would no longer be permitted to lounge or doze in the front lobby, but could only use the small, less comfortable and less elegant lounge in the back of the building with no view of comings and goings.

This new set of rules, and the boring food, was the final blow. Sara put a notice in mailboxes calling a residents' meeting. Residents signed a petition to S.O.B. which Sara and a committee delivered, but he explained that these mandates were from the corporate office and they would not change.

"We will move out," Sara said on behalf of the committee. "You can do that if you wish" said S.O.B. "But you will have to pay the monthly maintenance fee until we resell your unit, which may take some time. We have some of our unsold units left to sell first. And moving is expensive."

Sara shouted, "What do you mean we have to pay the monthly fee and wait for you to sell our units. We can't afford to pay for another place while you are doing that. We were promised that 90 percent of our pay-in would be refunded if we left."

"Only when we sell your unit," S.O.B. said. "And this could take a long time or forever. Another corporation, as you know, has built a large retirement complex nearby and they are competing with us. There are not enough retirees around who can afford these arrangements. I'm afraid we overbuilt for the market."

Sara and her friends were deeply depressed. They felt stuck. But Sara, in her usual creative way, began to improvise.

She told residents to show up at any of the meal times they wanted and sit where they wanted. Some people did have to wait for the next shift, and the shift numbers were uneven, but somehow everyone got fed. S.O.B. backed down on this rule.

Rule two was easy. Sara got everyone who owned a bathing suit to go into the pool on the Wednesday block of time. Even nonswimmers cooperated. They bought bathing suits or borrowed them from their children. Once the pool was packed, Sara called the town health department because the pool was over capacity. People also refused to leave the pool until S.O.B. came down personally and promised that there would be a lifeguard every day for two hours.

Breaking rule three was a lot of fun. Even

people who didn't usually frequent the lobby sat there all day for a week, even if they had to bring their own chairs. Prospective residents couldn't get through the lobby. Again S.O.B. backed down.

However, Sara and her accomplices were not satisfied. They had been told that when they sold their units they could move out and get 90 percent back whenever they wanted. They threatened to go on television and radio, and invited the newspapers to do stories locally as well as in the city of the corporate headquarters. People volunteered to look pathetic for photos. And they all threatened to move and not pay the maintenance fees.

"Take us to court," they said. It turned out that 16 of the residents had sons and daughters who were lawyers and that three had sons or daughters who were judges. Also, one woman had been a nanny for many years for the governor's children. Law students were recruited for pro bono representation.

S.O.B. and the corporation promised in writing to return the 90 percent when people left, but begged them to stay. "We are just one happy family" said S.O.B. "Sorry for the misunderstanding."

Sitting in her favorite lobby chair under the chandelier, Sara smiled smugly. She decided now that she had the residents organized, they might as well go to the state house to advocate for legislation curbing the abuses of HMOs and other insurance companies.

"Let's have a contest to rename this place," Sara suggested to S.O.B., who exhaustively agreed. The winning name was RASP's Nest, standing for Remarkably Aging Smart People's Nest.

Reverse Birthday Gifts

Giving Back As We Grow Older

November 15th is my birthday. I have instructed family and friends that I want no cards or presents. My mail carrier has enough to do delivering hordes of mail. By my age, a person is on every junk mail list in the country.

Giving to charities means that your name gets sold or swapped. I have enough unsolicited address labels to last until 2500 and I doubt if I will live that long. I also have enough unsolicited greeting cards sent by "causes" to take care of all my greeting card sending for a decade. I get so many travel brochures and credit card applications that I could make a sizable bonfire with them, especially if I include all the magazine subscription and insurance ads.

My only comfort when all this junk mail comes is that at least these "causes" and corporations are not telephoning me like so many others who solicit my business or charitable contributions at inconvenient times.

Now the reason I do not want any presents is that by my age a person has more stuff at home than there are places to put it. It is hard to part with stuff once it becomes yours, and so it is best not to add new things to the accumulation of years. I already have pocketbooks to match the too many clothes I have. My mantelpiece and shelves are already crowded with dust collectors.

I think at age seventy and thereafter we should have reverse birthday presents as a custom. The older person should give away to all friends and family unneeded possessions as gifts on our older birthdays.

I am against receiving birthday cards unless people feel an urgent need to send me the unsolicited greeting cards *they* got in the mail from causes and charities. Most commercial greetings for older birthdays are ageist, implying it is a joke, disgrace, or calamity to be old. As a gerontologist who sees the good side of aging, I do not appreciate cards that make it look as if elders spend their time snoozing, drinking, forgetting things, lying about their ages, and generally acting senile and silly.

My seventies so far have been mostly wonderful and I am proud and happy to have lived so long in a difficult society. Of course, I must admit that being seventy-eight is a little different than my previous seventies. At seventy-eight you realize suddenly that you are moving toward eighty. Seventy-five is mid-seventies. Seventy-eight does have a little different feel. I have a friend who has been seventy-nine for two years, perhaps fearing the prejudices against eighty-year-old people in a society that sees youth as good and old as a four-letter word.

I intend to continue to be outrageous in my late seventies, eighties, and for however long God gives me to live on this earth. I intend to make trouble for those who are ageist, sexist, racist, homophobic, or just plain mean, nasty, withholding, and evil. I glory in the fact that at my age I have freedom to speak out and there is very little that anyone can do to stop me.

I am extremely grateful that I am still teaching at a number of colleges. I learn from younger generations as I teach them. Young people are seldom gray haired and sometimes wear stiletto heels, which may cause bunions later in life. Young people cannot yet envision "grow old along with me, the best is yet to be."

One of the nice things about aging is you can wear comfortable shoes and sneakers all the time and nobody will care or probably even notice.

Here are some other nice things about aging:

1. You get to tell old jokes to new generations who never heard them. You can feel superior when they don't know about public events you have lived through.
2. You get a social security check monthly and now you can get it even if you are working and not have to pay back one dollar for every two dollars you earned that year over a limit.
3. You have Medicare, even with its imperfections.
4. You get senior discounts.
5. Hopefully, you have learned to say "No" to

things you don't want to do and "Yes" to things you want to do, even when they are considered unsuitable for your age.

6. You are firm in your identity and don't need to go looking for it like mid-life crisis folks.

7. If you are retired or semiretired, you can do your errands during the weekdays instead of weekends or evenings when the lines are long.

8. Unless you are caretaking a spouse or are one of the million American grandparents caring for grandchildren, you are not responsible for others. Your time is yours.

9. We live in times when there are many aids as some of the detriments of aging occur. There are books on tape and large type books (like this one) and magazines if our vision is not as good as it once was. There are hearing aids. There are devices we can use to cope with infirmities. For example, there are aids to help with arthritis, fibromyalgia, osteoporosis, and back problems. These are in a free catalogue, Living Better with Arthritis. Call 1-800-654-0707 or write Aids for Arthritis, 35 Wakefield Drive, Medford, NH 08055. One great idea is the elastic shoelaces—you only have to tie them once.

10. We also get to exercise our minds and rest our bodies.

11. In retirement we can take advantage of early bird specials in restaurants and get cheap lunches at senior centers.

12. People will carry bundles for us, open doors, tie our shoelaces, and generally help us if we ask for it or put on a pitiful face. I have been known to do this just to make young people feel good and worthy without it costing them money.

13. In writing our memoirs or telling our reminiscences, we can invent, exaggerate, or otherwise enhance ourselves. The ultimate of this was a woman of eighty-plus in my summer memoir writing course. She was into past lives, and wrote about herself as Isis of Egypt and other historical characters. As my friend Wendyl Ross noted when I told her, "It is fascinating how those who believe in past lives were always someone famous, not just an ordinary person."

Be extraordinary in your late years. Celebrate birthdays. Give away useless stuff.

It's *Your* Brain—Use It or Lose It

Older women have ingenuity and creativity. Examples are everywhere and I want to share some that I came across recently.

At a meeting of the Massachusetts Poetry Association, I chatted with Marie Rimi of Everett, a woman I had known for years as a poet and active member of the association. I discovered that she saw a need that older women have and found a way to meet that need and earn herself some money while doing it.

Marie, who loved to sew, realized that women living in assisted living and long-term care communities experience what many of us older women do—our body size and shape changes. We grow wider and thinner and we may get shorter due to bone shrinkage. Our clothes are too small, too big, or too long. Marie called the activity directors at seven establishments to introduce her business, which she cleverly called Perfect Fit. She offered to come do fittings and alterations. Her offer was accepted and she has been doing this work for five years.

Many of her clients had beloved clothes acquired on their travels that she could "remodel" for them. In addition, she has made friends of the residents and enjoys listening to their stories about how they got their garments and other matters.

She applauded when an elder had her take a beautiful velvet stole with a pink lining and cut it into four smaller stoles for each of the woman's daughters to wear. What a wonderful legacy!

The next woman I would like to tell about got the idea of celebrating being sixty by going around the world in sixty days. She used her savings and gifts from family and friends to take a remarkable trip. Then she wrote all about her experiences and reflections in a book, *East Toward Dawn: A Woman's Solo Journey Around the World*. I love that she pointed out "one of the benefits of traveling alone is having the freedom to make decisions without the need to compromise with companions on how to proceed." She also said, "The art of dining alone is underrated. Without the need to converse with a companion, the single diner can be attentive to the fine food and surroundings and can allow her mind to wander at will … eavesdrop on the conversations of those around and enjoy the paintings on the walls."

However, the book is much more than a travel memoir because it offers the author's observations and wisdom about life and the human spirit plus humor.

When I taught memoir writing at a senior center, I discovered the creativity of Loretta Petrilli of Franklin, Massachusetts. She makes charming gray-haired dolls. One of the class members gifted me with a doll in a purple dress and red hat as in the poem by Jenny Joseph that begins, "When I Am an Old Woman I Shall Wear Purple." The doll sits on my mantle to remind me of the fine crafts older women make.

Another doll maker is Wilmington, Massachusetts, resident Nancy Cronin, who makes dolls of old women. Nancy has always liked creating crafts. Twenty years ago she used to do broomstick witch dolls and her mother suggested she "make old women look pretty instead of like witches." So now Nancy makes interesting old character dolls. A recent example was Miss Havisham from Charles Dickens' *Great Expectations*. She made Miss Havisham in her wedding dress worn for twenty-five years after her fiancé dumped her. Nancy shows her dolls at assisted living places and also exhibits at doll shows.

Certainly men are creative too. At eighty-nine, Daniel Fogel of Lincoln, Massachusetts, is both a sculptor and a poet. He enrolled in my poetry class and wrote poems that made class members laugh at his wit and learn from his profound thoughts.

Among creative elders are men and women who reside in nursing homes. The stereotypes about nursing home residents are combated in a remarkable book by Charles Tindell, *Seeing Beyond the Wrinkles: Stories of Ageless Courage, Humor and Faith*. Tindell, the chaplain at a nursing home, has written moving stories about residents whose lives can help us face our own aging and that of loved ones. Tindell says, "We need to recognize and celebrate humor and quickness of wit among the elderly to affirm such attributes as gifts of God and let them know we appreciate these gifts they share with us." He cites many humorous remarks by nursing home residents and points out that we need to listen to and learn from the reminiscences of old people.

Do see beyond the wrinkles in yourself and others.

People-Watching

Good, Cheap Fun

Being a sociologist, your Dr. Ruth has always been fascinated by the public behavior of people. And, as a gerontologist and older person herself, she is especially interested in the public behavior of seasoned citizens.

One great site for observing the behavior of people including older persons is my town recycling area, more popularly called the Wellesley dump. A group of retirees who are sort of recycling hobbyists hang out at the "take it or leave it" area where residents deposit or retrieve what they determine to be still-usable items. A bunch of retired men, perhaps to get away from boredom or their wives, socialize there watching for treasures or just plain usable stuff. They also exchange pleasantries and the news of the day. They even bring coffee.

An older woman, known to some as "The Dragon Lady of the Dump," also hangs out, swooping down on the incoming cars and avidly beating others to the valuable finds. Many find her too competitive and wonder what she does with all she takes. The hypothesis is that she resells the goods at garage sales or to dealers. However, another woman, somewhat younger, is known to some as "The Angel of the Dump," as she is kind enough to help frail people lift heavy items into their cars.

In a separate area, under cover, the Wellesley recycling area also has book shelves in a building wall where people can take or leave books. One old woman comes and fills her car to capacity with so many books that others sometimes resent this. However, once when I was looking for books for some low-income children, I gently approached the book lady with my search efforts and she graciously dug an appropriate assortment from her car for me.

In case any of my readers are now excited about going to get freebies at the Wellesley dump, I must warn them that one has to be a Wellesley resident with a recycling facility sticker. I hear from my friends from Weston that the dump in that town has an even more elegant take-and-leave place. Again, you will have to move to Weston and get a sticker to enjoy the discards of that town. Perhaps your town has a similar facility.

Another public place where I have been observing seasoned citizens and the habits of others is the Natick Longfellow Sports Club to which I belong. People there become rather territorial about their swimming lanes. One older woman whom I think of as the managerial type is very explicit about telling others where they ought to swim. Timidity, bravado, selfishness, and other human traits are exhibited. One male swimmer who prefers a certain lane will take that over, displacing any person already immersed in that lane. He even whacks them with aggressive strokes. If crowded conditions require lane sharing, some will politely ask if they can share, but others just plunge in.

I am also fascinated by restaurant behavior. Recently, I observed four women who had lunched together. When the check came, one got out a calculator and figured to the penny what each owed for the meal, including tax and tip. This was followed by a time consuming effort to verify what each person had ordered. I contrast this with the custom of my friends who just split the check and tip by the number of diners, not to worry about the differences. We figure it all evens out in the long run.

Supermarket behavior is interesting. A man complained to me that he does not like to be in the check out line behind elders because they take too long. He resents our slowness in putting stuff on the belts, getting out coupons and money. He was a bit put off when I suggested that he might consider helping us unload our carriages.

Additionally, I like to watch older people with their pets. Those who walk dogs are usually considerate of others by carrying plastic bags into which they scoop the deposits of their animals. I must admit that some senior citizens carry baggies in their purses and pockets for other reasons.

At senior centers and other places where refreshments are served, they will often grab food. Sometimes this is because of low income and other times it verges on a need to be given something in a world perceived to not be very giving. I have also seen people of all ages remove magazines from doctor's offices and waiting rooms. I must confess that I once tore out an article that I wanted to share with my students. Nobody is perfect, not even me.

Having confessed to imperfection, I will tell a story on myself. I, who never bought a lottery ticket in my life, recently won a ticket as a door prize. My first impulse was to tear it up or give it away, but I admit that I asked the person next to me at the table what to do with it. He showed me how to scratch it with a coin and told me I had won four dollars. He said to take it to any place where lottery tickets are sold to redeem the ticket. This anti-gambling zealot did just that. I felt like a hypocrite.

As long as I'm in a confessional mood, I will tell another tale of my misdeeds. Recently, when a tractor trailer rig overturned, I was stuck in a traffic jam at rush hour. I was able to creep in the breakdown lane to an exit which lead to a lovely hotel. As I always have a bathing suit in the car, I went into the hotel, had a refreshing swim in the indoor pool, and followed it up with a warm shower. All free. By the time I returned to the road, the traffic jam was cleared. The nice thing about being a senior citizen is that nobody in the hotel ever suspected that I was a "crasher."

Doing outrageous things is fun. Maybe some staid readers might want to make a resolution to be at least a little more outrageous. But we do have to watch our public behavior so as not to give elders a bad name. Ageist people are always ready for negative stereotyping. We don't want to give them any more ammunition.

We can be bold when we are old. But we need to be considerate of others and help give old age a good name. I hope readers will enjoy their aging. After all, the alternative to aging is not good.

Limit Yourself To One Yard Sale Each Weekend

Here is advice from Karen Brooks of Destin, Florida, who graciously wrote that she liked my chapter on economizing in my book *Be An Outrageous Older Woman*. She added, and gave me permission to relay to others, a list of questions she has developed over the years to help her get the most from her money. Her self-queries follow:

Before you decide to buy:
- Can I do without it?
- Can I use something I already have?
- Can I do it myself?
- Can I make it?
- Can I fix something to work (revamp, remodel)?
- Can I substitute? Is there an inexpensive alternative?
- Can I borrow it?
- Can I solve the problem cheaper?
- Can I get it free?
- Can I trade it for labor?

After you decide to buy:
- Can I get it cheaper at the source?
- Can I get it secondhand?
- How often will I use it? Can I justify the cost or would I be better to do without it?

- What is the cost of upkeep? Are there incidental expenses?
- How will I store it? How will I move it?
- Is there something else that will do this job and others and will be more useful in the future?
- What are my long-term versus short-term needs?

Before buying a specific item:
- What do I want to accomplish? What do I want to do? Are my expectations realistic?
- Have I looked it over carefully? Have I tested it?
- How long will it last? Is it durable?
- Is it good quality? For my purposes, is good quality justified?
- How long can I use it? Does it have other uses now or in the future?

To Karen's excellent questions, I would like to add a postscript. Some of us have thought we were getting bargains by shopping at garage sales. The price is usually great but we run the hazard of cluttering up our houses. Having managed to clutter up mine with garage sale treasures, I have had to discipline myself to one garage sale each weekend.

I have also learned from Patricia Shotwell of Weston, Massachusetts, a trick to de-clutter my house. Her method is to fill one grocery or paper or plastic bag a day with things you can get rid of by giving or throwing them away. Patsy admits that she sometimes finds herself at ten at night searching for unneeded stuff to fulfill her self-imposed daily quota. Patsy's system works if you adhere to it. Her plan reminds me of the *Boston Globe* Confidential Chat writer who four decades ago recommended a person spend twenty minutes a day cleaning some mess in their home. The limitation of one bag or twenty minutes may make cleaning or de-cluttering bearable to some.

Besides feeling guilty about the clutter accumulated with all our years of living, some older people feel embarrassed that they have not kept up to date with all the new technology. For them, I offer my message from the wrong side of the digital divide.

I write books on a typewriter. I use "snail mail," not e-mail. I don't fax. I call on a wired telephone and never call while driving. I play tapes on an old tape recorder and read real books held on my lap, rather than on a laptop screen. I go to the supermarket myself instead of ordering by computer to be delivered and shelved. I have a relationship with a bank teller, not an ATM. I browse in bookstores and libraries instead of ordering books on-line. And worst offense of all—I talk to old friends and new ones, in their homes or mine, or restaurants. I don't reveal all to strangers on web sites and chat rooms. I even lie that my phone is not touch tone so I don't have to punch in many numbers. But I have never lost a word I wrote and have a quite satisfactory life. So there.

Americans generally are having love affairs with technology, feeling they have to master and buy every new product. However, some of us can enjoy nature and the simple things in life.

Fearing Retirement?

Two of the most important decisions in life are when to retire and how to spend your retirement years. The timing decision is simple for some people with ill health, dislike of their jobs, or concrete plans to do something exciting. For them, retirement is a welcome alternative. For others, love of their jobs or financial considerations may make them want to postpone the Big R.

However, there is a middle category of individuals who are ambivalent about retirement because they don't know what it will bring.

Are you in terror you'll soon make an error
retire too soon or feel its doom
fear being ignored or being bored?

Well, for all three types of people, here are some tips for retirement that people have found useful. The tips are based on Dr. Barbara H. Vinick's research. Dr. Vinick, who lives in Swampscott, Massachusetts, prepared these tips for a talk to faculty and staff at Salem State College, and graciously is allowing me to use them. She was my Ph.D. student at Boston University's sociology department and now works at the Bedford Veteran's Administration Normative Aging Study and at Brandeis University, and she also heads Mature Focus, an organization that does research on mature consumers.

Tips for Retirement
Based on Interviews with Retirees

1. At first, ambivalence about retirement is commonplace. Being at loose ends, missing friends at work, lacking a sense of purpose, and missing the authority you exercised are not rare. Realize that as the weeks and months pass, you will establish a new routine that is satisfying to you.

2. Set realistic agendas for accomplishments after retirement. Don't be afraid to go at a slower pace, and relax. Some people set such ambitious schedules for themselves that they feel guilty that they aren't accomplishing enough, that they're falling behind. It is natural to use more time if you have it. Go easy on yourself.

3. Retirement does not provide make-overs for dispositions and preferences. Don't expect to change dramatically the kinds of things that you or your spouse like to do. Most people continue to take pleasure in pursuits and interests they have developed over the years. Take time now to think about what sparks your enthusiasm. There are many ways to be happy in retirement.

4. That said, be open to new experiences. Try something new, perhaps something you've thought about but never had time to pursue— traveling, sailing, painting, sewing. Even if you've had a disappointing experience in the

past, try again. You may be pleasantly surprised.

5. Expect that you will feel better after you retire.
   You will have more time to exercise, better
   opportunity to eat properly, and experience less
   stress. But don't deny health problems if they
   should arise. You'll have more time to look after
   yourself and deal with medical issues. If a
   health condition affects your activities, dwell on
   what you *can* do, not what you can't do.

6. Think and plan carefully about finances in
   retirement, but realize that expenses often
   decrease—for clothing and transportation, for
   example.

7. If you are retired and your spouse is still working, problematic issues may be more likely to
   crop up. Take the time to discuss expectations
   of each other. Housework should be an area of
   special consideration.

8. Enjoy time together with your partner, but
   make time for activities on your own and with
   others. Guilt that the other person is "home
   alone" is usually unwarranted.

9. Retirement allows more time for other family
   members. Decide and come to consensus with
   the amount of help and care you give to other
   generations—children, grandchildren, and parents. Consider your needs, as well as others'. If
   problems seem too difficult, seek outside help.

10. Housework deserves special attention from

couples after retirement. Negotiation may be required as to who does what, when it gets done, and how.

11. Volunteer your time. Retired people are a tremendous, often untapped, resource for our country! The abilities, talents, strengths, and wisdom that you've acquired through the years are needed by our communities. It is often said, and true: You will gain as much as you give. You *will* find a volunteer activity that you feel comfortable doing, that needs doing, and that makes you feel good doing it.

12. Working part-time after you retire is neither advisable nor inadvisable. It's entirely up to you. If you need the money, or the structure, or the work environment, or the sense of purpose, go for it. But people can be just as satisfied not doing paid work after they retire.

13. Features that enhance marriage in retirement are the same that enhance marriage at other stages of life: knowledge of yourself and your partner based on reality and not wishful thinking; respect for your partner's characteristics, and the differences in preferences, views, and opinions that every couple is bound to have; a spirit of compromise that fosters both self-fulfillment and concession for the sake of the other's happiness.

14. If you're single, make a special effort to substitute relationships you've developed at work

with relationships with friends and family members. Initiate meetings and activities; get out of the house.

15.Some people are excited about making a new start in a different place after retiring, and some cannot imagine pulling up stakes. Consider not only the climate and the housing options, but also whether you will find people who share your interests and lifestyle. If you know people who have already moved to the area you have in mind, or are familiar with the place yourself, so much the better. Sometimes it takes a while to feel comfortable in a new environment, so plan to give yourself time to adjust.

Humor

Humor has many functions. It counteracts sadness and madness, relieves tension, stimulates physiologically and psychologically, and reputedly aids wellness and recovery from illness. Moreover, it promotes solidarity by shared laughter or smiles. It allows you to attack aggressors, enemies, and superordinates in safe, subtle ways. Humor also raises the self esteem of the humorist because it elicits smiles, laughter, applause, and other positive responses.

Humor can also help overcome fear by joking about what one fears, thus making it less scary. It is therefore a viable and acceptable defense. It is the last refuge of the powerless, and many old people feel powerless these days, when services are being cut and medical care is being mismanaged to deprive elders of resources.

Therefore, it is not surprising that those who are old, those who fear getting old, and those who work with the old often joke about aging. Jokes about aging circulate very rapidly. They appear in writing or in the voice of a speaker and soon are told and retold with the original jokester forgotten and not credited.

For example, a story circulated everywhere about the older woman who told her friends she was remarrying after widowhood. Her friends asked if he was interesting and she said, "No." They asked if he had money and the answer was again negative, as was the answer to whether he was handsome. But then the bride-to-be said, "But he still drives at night."

Many old people and those who will soon be old fear the loss of driving acuity and the freedom and independence that driving provides. Therefore, it is no surprise that this joke made the rounds.

Similarly, a few years ago the joke of the year was about an old man who went to the doctor complaining that he couldn't hear in one ear. The doctor said, "You are eighty years old—what do you expect?" The man replied, "But my other ear is eighty years old too. Would you mind having a look at my ear?" Another version of the story referred to a bad knee, but the reason both versions of the story became so popular was the same. Old people fear superficial and ageist doctors who trivialize elders' symptoms. The joke was an attack on such doctors and ventilation for elders' fears of poor medical care.

It has amazed me that I am often introduced as a humorous speaker and invited to speak because the inviter has heard I make audiences laugh. Actually, I make many points I consider to be fairly important and serious, but that is not what my audiences or readers remember. Although I have had a number of papers in scholarly journals, the greatest number of requests for reprints has come for an article on His and Her Aging. The reasons for that is that in it I included a lengthy piece of doggerel that was fairly humorous about the differences between men and women who are old.

In the same vein, the humorous part of my best-selling *Be an Outrageous Older Woman* are often commented on instead of the many serious points in that book. People are desperate for humor about aging because Americans so fear being old.

Gene Cohen, M.D., a George Washington University psychiatrist who has much of importance to communicate about therapy for elders is often quoted for his jokes rather than his theories. Also, psychiatrist Martin Berezin, M.D., founder of the Boston Society for Gerontologic Psychiatry, is famed for his humor perhaps more than his many profound contributions.

There are so many jokes about aging in America because we, as a youth-oriented society, fear aging. It would be interesting to do cross-cultural research to see if the amount of joking about aging correlates with the degrees of gerontophobia and ageism in various societies.

Humor as a safety valve is functional, but it would perhaps be healthier if people did not so much fear aging that it becomes a joke. This is especially true because some of the jokes about aging do the elderly a great disservice. They poke fun at the old and add to the stereotypes of the aged as silly, senile, confused, and incompetent. Many of these jokes are about the supposed lack of memory of old people and their supposed child-like or nasty behavior. This adds to the fear of aging and to the reluctance to associate with old people. At seventy-eight, I may be unduly sensi-tive to these jokes denigrating me and my age peers, and I will not repeat examples of them here for fear they will be spread about even more. Sadly, the majority of these jokes satirize older women. This reflects societal bias.

Try to come to acceptance of your aging. If you joke about a "senior moment" when you forget, you are implying elders are the only forgetful ones. People of all ages forget, not just old people. Keep your sense of humor but remember being old is a life stage, not a joke.

Safe Driving Renewal

Remember how when we were children, we loved April Fool's Day because we could make a statement, and when someone responded, we would say "April Fool" and laugh. I remember this as I write. I also remember the cliché "there is no fool like an old fool."

Well, it is fun to be a bit foolish, not overserious, at any age, but it is a good idea not to be an old fool. Most of us are pretty wise because we have lived a long time, but there are a few of us who are fools.

One variety of fool is the older person who refuses to take the 55 Alive Mature Driving course. I took this course recently and was shocked when people in the class reported they had told their friends about it, but the friends insisted they already knew how to drive and didn't need to take the course. The friends were foolish because as we age we have some decrements in hearing, vision, and reaction time that make it important for us to learn how to compensate for these.

The eight dollars the course costs is a bargain because you get eight hours of good instruction, a fine ninety-four-page workbook, a copy of the state drivers' license manual, and even have some fun during the course.

The instructors are volunteers. Our instructor

was Dr. Harold Homefield of Sudbury, Massachusetts, a retired speech pathologist and educator. He was an experienced, competent, and humorous instructor. Like other volunteers, Dr. Homefield was trained by the American Association for Retired Persons, which sponsors the course. It is recommended that older drivers take the course every few years, so this was the second time I took the course, having taken it about five years ago.

Perhaps you might even want to volunteer to be trained to teach the course. Actually, since I have my name in the AARP volunteer bank, I have been called to train to teach the course, but declined because I am busy teaching in other areas.

The 55 Alive program reimburses volunteers for their program-related authorized out-of-pocket expenses, including such costs as mileage, parking, postage, and basic supplies. There are currently five thousand volunteer instructors who teach the course throughout the USA and another thousand volunteers who coordinate various aspects of the program in their geographic locations. If you would like to be a 55 Alive volunteer, write to 55 Alive, 601 E Street, NW, Washington, DC 20049. Should you want to find out where and when there will be a course near you, call the AARP program resources department.

Some of the things covered in the course are a self-assessment; vision, hearing, and driver calisthenics; normal driving situations; hazardous driving environments; driver guidance; the vehicle; alcohol and medications as they impact on driving; and driving decisions.

If you complete the course, you get a certificate (there are no examinations). In some states, you can get a discount off car insurance for taking the course.

In the driving course, I discovered that two major problems for older drivers are knowing when they have the right of way and making a left hand turn. I found out some of my bad habits were driving when tired, driving at rush hours, looking at a map or directions when driving, and eating or drinking while driving. Other people also found out their bad habits and how to overcome them. Do you have any bad driving habits?

There are some people who believe older drivers should be road tested after a certain age. Others disagree, believing this is age discrimination. They maintain that all people who have accidents should be road tested. Actually, more accidents are caused by very young drivers than older drivers. But as older drivers, we need to be responsible and give up our licenses when we can no longer drive safely. This is a very hard thing to do, and a lot of denial is involved. A compromise is that many older drivers drive only during daylight hours, only in dry road conditions, and only in local, familiar, non-rush-hour circumstances.

To help older people it is very important that

cities and towns provide transportation for those who cannot drive. Some people when they age and cannot drive any longer make the decision to move near public transportation. But it is hard for people sometimes to give up homes in suburbs where they have lived for a long time. This is why it is important to know about resources.

Whether you are driving carefully and mindfully or being driven, your Dr. Ruth wishes you good things in your destination. Don't be a fool in April or any other month.

Of Course We Are "Weirder"— We've Had More Time To Practice

By the time you are old, you have met many weird people. Let me tell you about some I remember. There was the woman who had ten cats, and had all ten of them sleep in bed with her. There were the people last summer who went on the three hours senior's boat ride and had the bad judgment to "pig out" at the $6 all-you-can-eat greasy breakfast buffet on the boat. When the turbulence began – well, I guess I don't have to go any further. I was rather proud of my wiser choice of a bagel and orange juice. Actually though, seasoned citizens are no more weird than younger people.

Unfortunately, if we are a bit strange, they blame it on our age because of the stereotypes about aging. It is a good idea to carry a few marbles in your pocket or purse so if they imply you have lost some, you can empty your pockets and declare "Not yet!"

I certainly can confess to being weird myself, but I WILL keep quiet about some crimes I am currently committing.

My car is testimony to my eccentricity. Here is a list of things living in my car:
- A bathing suit, towel and shampoo should I

swim at my sports club or pass a luxurious hotel where I crash its pool for variety and challenge;

- Various sized plastic bags for rained on treasures at the town dump "take and leave" area which furnishes my home, fills my bookshelves, and yields gifts;

- Multiple maps and magnifying glass, boxes of my books and book ads to make sales, clean underwear and toothbrush for unexpected overnighters;

- A pen and notebook for directions or poems erupting while driving; sunglasses with sidebars for blinding solar glare, and incognito stops when I'm messy;

- A magazine, newspaper or book to occupy myself in waiting rooms, juices and herb teas for caffeine-only places, a thick pillow for roadside naps;

- Water bottle, toll change, sunblock, raincoat and hat, flashlight, cleansing towelettes for a dirty world, and a tall plastic sunflower for my antenna in huge, crowded parking lots;

My daughter hates my lair,
critics peer in my car and sneer
not knowing what I do or hold dear.
They probably have clean desks too,
with creative moments few

Some people think old people are all alike. As a gerontologist, I can tell you that is false. The research shows that the older we get, the more we are different because we have had longer to get that way. In other words, ten- or twenty-year-olds are more like age peers than seventy- and eighty-year-olds. We each have our own special personalities and ways of acting developed through long and varied experiences.

It is interesting also that in old age, as research has demonstrated, men exhibit some nurturing and expressive behaviors that at younger ages are more characteristic of females. Conversely, women in later years exhibit some of the more assertive and even aggressive roles characteristic of younger men. Each gender does somewhat of a role reversal. Retired men who never were into domestic roles take up cooking, home chores and nurturing of grandchildren, perhaps making up for a time when they couldn't. Women, in later years, have taken more active and instrumental roles in advocacy. I don't mean to imply that there is anything weird about this phenomena. It is rather nice that some people can switch modalities.

It is fascinating to observe also how people may change their style of clothing as they age. Some who dressed conservatively during their working years, may branch out in retirement into flamboyancy and bright colors. I am one of those. Once I wore navy, black and brown dresses. Now I wear pants and tops in wild colors like my purple and pink "Outrageous Older Woman" t-shirts and flowing, bright colored shawls.

The older years can be the fun years and the years of not being reticent to say who we really are. So readers, age outrageously and courageously. Be weird if you like. In young years, the opinions of others are most important to us. In our later years, how we feel about ourselves is the most important. We have earned the right to be eccentric as long as it does no harm. Better eccentric than bland and dull. We can dress for humor instead of for success. What are they going to do to us if we speak our minds?

Enjoy your aging.

The Ups and Downs of Aging Courageously

As a gerontologist and sociologist, I write and lecture on how to age outrageously and courageously, but sometimes I feel like a hypocrite. While at 78 I love being a seasoned citizen, even I suffer from the losses associated with aging. Many seasoned citizens suffer from two kinds of ageism. External ageism means we are discriminated against and thought to be stupid because we are old. Internalized ageism means that we lose self esteem, thinking we are less competent and less interesting now that we are older.

For public appearances I wear my tee-shirt in purple with pink lettering that says "Outrageous Older Woman." I also carry a tote bag which shouts RASP, an acronym I invented for Remarkable Aging Smart People, or Ravishing Aging Sexy Person, or Radically Aging Stressed Person. I also wear buttons that say such things as "Youth Is A Gift of Nature: Aging Is A Work of Art" and "Aged to Perfection." I also put on a flamboyant collection of hats to demonstrate metaphorically that we can put on wonderful new hats as we age.

Secretly, I know that chronic and acute illnesses, like my own osteoporosis, arthritis and tachycardia are not joyous, especially in the current mean, lean, and obscene medical care system. Also, we lose friends and relatives and dread reading the obituary page for fear that we will find our peers there. Many of us grieve spouses and deal with living alone late in life.

Recently I counted and discovered I had written in the last few years fifty-seven poems as well as a book of doggerel on the good aspects of aging, such as wisdom, freedom from responsibilities, and time for fun, travel, and creativity. But in darker moments, I have also written items such as the following:

> If you can locate a bathroom
> everywhere you're going to be
> longer than an hour
> and can get away with calling people darling
> or pal
> because you can't remember their names
> and have enough money or know good thrift
> shops
> and don't snore when you catnap in public
> and love the color gray
> and have wild hats to cover thinning hair
> and love wakes and funerals and prefer soft
> foods to steak
> and have a lot of chutzpah to stare down
> ageist folks
> and have a doctor who has smarts, time and a
> heart
> then you can age maybe outrageously and
> courageously.

What inspired the poem is that I took two friends in their seventies to a day on older women's health sponsored by the Center for Women and Aging at Brandeis University. Both friends have health issues and I thought they would benefit from the physicians and scientists who spoke. But there I sat with the two friends sleeping on either side of me through much of the program.

We get scared – no *terrified* – when we see those our own age or older losing alertness or becoming forgetful, or even demented. We worry if our energy or brain power will suffice for our lifetime. We also brood that our money will not last.

It is interesting that as some people age, they become very tight with their money while others are profligate, figuring they can't take it with them. Although I have enough funds to heat my house in the winter, I find myself turning down the thermostat and then must remind myself of the risks of hypothermia. I am generous with my adult children, but cheap when it comes to spending money on myself.

Elders experience the hostility of younger generations who feel we are too costly to the society and too slow on the roads and walkways. I often experience obscene gestures and nagging horns blaring from younger drivers who resent that I take a few extra seconds at a difficult intersection or when parking. People appear to be impatient at the checkout lines as we unload our carts perhaps too slowly.

I find antagonizing or confronting such people only reinforces their prejudice that older people are dumb and difficult. Humor works better.

Of course we can't deal with the death of a loved one by joking. However we mourn we can recognize the living have to live and the dead would not want them to jump into the grave with them. I like the Chinese custom of bringing a bit of food to the cemetery at burial, symbolic that the living have to eat to go on.

I have lost several friends in recent years through death and have worked to make new friends. The new friends do not replace the old ones, but they do provide the support network and community I require.

Perhaps one of the greatest benefits of longevity is that you have the opportunity to revisit good experiences in your life and resolve bad ones. I have been teaching memoir and poetry writing courses to seasoned citizens and have discovered how marvelous it is for people to reexperience life by writing. Elders in my classes have loved sharing about the good times. They have been comforted and supported by others in the class as they have shared their sad times and losses through writing. One woman had been depressed because she felt that every time she had made a major decision or chosen a path in her life, it had been the wrong choice. When she wrote her memoir, she found that she had made the only possible choice given the context of her life, society, and the times. She forgave herself for the alleged mistakes and her depression lifted.

A man whose father was killed in Normandy in World War II constructed a memoir of his father through records, letter, photos, and interviews of those who knew his father. This was of enormous comfort to the man who was four years old when his father died, to mourn and then memorialize him as a hero.

For me and countless others, old age brings a flowering of creativity. My first book was published when I was fifty-five and I have had eight more books since. For those of us whose lives were crowded with work, family, and doing for others, old age gives us time to reflect and share our hard earned wisdom.

Also, what can they do to us if we speak up and assert our rights and views? We can be politically active because we have the time to nag politicians by phone and letter. This helps vent a lot of anger. Despite the difficulties, we can really be outrageous and courageous. It is better than being passive and puny. Outrageous means coming out of rage by getting our needs met and working to improve society in the tradition of tribal elders in more communal times.

Exploring

October is when we celebrate Christopher Columbus, an explorer. Those of us who are retired may have, for the first time in our lives, time to explore our environment and beyond. Maybe we can even take time to explore our inner selves. This essay gives you some suggestions for that exploration.

Explore your childhood and share it with your descendents. Write some reminiscences. Since our sensory impressions remain with us as triggers to experience, here is a trick to get you started writing. Put on a piece of paper the line I can still hear, or the line I can still see, or the line I can still taste. Or the line I can still smell. See what comes to mind and then write about it. You may be surprised.

Explore your years by writing some of the following: my first car was ___, my first job was ___, my favorite teacher was ___, my least favorite teacher was___, my best friend was ___, my first date was ___, my child's birth was ___, and so forth. See what memories come up and write about them.

Explore what it feels like to keep a journal. Buy a notebook and try everyday to write some thought you have. Don't worry about style. Just put down what comes to mind. You will be fascinated at what comes up.

Explore indoor gardening in the winter. Many of us seasoned citizens are on low sodium diets. Growing herbs indoors can supply you with tasty seasoning for your food so that you will not miss salt.

Explore some new kind of exercises to keep you conditioned.

Explore increasing your vocabulary. Flip through the dictionary until you find an unfamiliar word that interests you. Use it three times in speaking and/or writing. Then you will own that word. It is easy to get into the habit of using the same words all the time. Boring!

Explore all the services your city or town offers older people. Maybe you don't need them now, but it will be good to have a folder about them in case you need them later or a friend or relative does. Start with your Council on Aging and Senior Center.

Explore ways to give your feet a lift. Many older people have weak or fallen arches and the pain spreads from the balls of your feet to your heels, your ankles, your legs and even your lower back. You can have custom made orthotics shoe inserts made by podiatrists or you can buy ready-made ones. I did and they helped me.

Explore your own closets and drawers. At our ages we have usually accumulated a lot of stuff we will never use or have forgotten about. When I have explored my closets, I have found some clothes I need to give away and others that I can use in creative new ways. For instance, I have found dresses that can be cut at the waist to make new tops or to make new skirts. Instead of going shopping for clothes, try shopping in your own closet to see what can be recycled. Less crowded closets and drawers also mean the remaining clothes won't get wrinkled because stuff is no longer squashed together.

Explore your jewelry. Often pins and beads that you don't seem to wear can take on a whole new life if you attach the pin to the bottom of a pair of beads to make a designer piece by you. An earring with a mate gone can also be attached to a chain or necklace to make a self-designed piece. If you have had the odd earring for over a year, its unlikely that its mate will ever turn up.

Explore your crowded bookcases. Why are you accumulating dust on books you will never read again? Give them away to friends, relatives, a library, or the "take and leave" place if your town has one at its dump. This will make space to accumulate other books you may never read ... ha-ha.

Explore, if you are depressed, how to get help, because help is available. You can get a free pamphlet "How to Talk to Your Doctor About Depression and Be Well Again" from the National Council on Aging, 409 Third St., SW, Washington, D.C. 20024, or on the Web at www.ncoa.org. A video is also available from NCOA. It is called "The Many

Faces of Depression." Another organization, the American Society on Aging, offers a community education and screening program for clinical depression. This is called "The Blues: Not a Normal Part of Aging" and can be obtained by your senior center or other community organization. There is no charge. They can be contacted at 853 Market Street, Suite 511, San Francisco, CA 94103–1824, or on the Web at www.asaging.org.

Explore working if you need money or structure in your life. Many employers who used to ignore older would-be employees are now courting them. Explore your creativity. Recently, Providence, RI, artist Riva Leviten sent me a postcard she had made by cutting a postcard sized piece of cardboard out of a cereal box, using the blank side for writing and a stamp. It was a colorful, recycled, economical, and clever item. She also told me about a fabulous group in Providence at the Tockwotten Home who call themselves Sassy Seniors. Think about organizing some Sassy Seniors in your area.

Your creativity will suggest many more explorations than offered here. Also, remember that when Columbus discovered America he was really trying to get to the East Indies, or what was then called that. As you explore, serendipity may lead you in unexpected ways to new destinations. The main thing is to be in an exploring, not a stagnant, mode.

Mother-in-Law/Daughter-in-Law Relationships

Many readers are about the age of the Wellesley College Class of 1961, which asked me to speak at their recent reunion on the topic of getting along with adult sons and daughters and their spouses. I was informed that these women had a special interest in the problematic relationships between mothers-in-law and daughters-in-law.

Since I suspect readers might also be interested in this topic, I present some of the unfortunate mother-in-law and daughter-in-law tensions. I thank my friend Ellie Mamber for some suggestions of the role difficulties. Most of the bad scenarios have come from my observation and interviewing.

Certainly many mothers-in-law and daughters-in-law get along well, but I wish to help those who may not and have absorbed negative stereotypes of each other, contaminating interactions.

MIL (mother-in-law): I will give DIL (daughter-in-law) the benefit of my experience by giving her advice and suggestions.

DIL: My MIL is manipulative and her advice is rotten and outdated.

MIL: I hope, expect, or dread that DIL will be like my own daughter.

DIL: I hope, expect, or dread that MIL will be like my own mother.

MIL: My son is unhappy because DIL is neurotic, selfish, not meeting his needs, and not taking good care of him. She is worse than other DILs.

DIL: My MIL spoiled my husband so that he is neurotic, selfish, and doesn't meet my needs or take good care of me. She is worse than other MILs.

MIL: My grandchildren's problems are the fault of DIL who didn't (or doesn't) bring them up right. My daughter is a better mother.

DIL: My children's problems are the result of poor fathering because MIL failed to bring up her son to be a good father. MIL also pays more attention to her daughter's children than mine.

MIL: My DIL resents my attention to the grandchildren and tries to prevent a close relationship between me and them. She lets her mother be closer to the children.

DIL: My MIL is a bad influence on her grandchildren. I wish she would not bribe them with gifts and want to spend so much time with them. I hate when my MIL criticizes the way I bring up my children or relate to them as adults.

MIL is ashamed of DIL because of her failings, background, education, appearance. MIL cannot understand how her son could have chosen this woman to be his wife and is not completely able to conceal this.

DIL is ashamed of MIL because of her background, education, appearance, skills, etc. She cannot understand how her husband could have come from this family and knows her MIL resents her.

MIL expects DIL to become part of her extended family and fit in.

DIL expects her husband to become part of her extended family and fit in.

MIL always makes an effort to say the right thing, not to criticize or even make suggestions. She is always on guard.

DIL thinks MIL is a perfectionist, secretive, and uncommunicative.

MIL finds DIL's house so unappealing that she keeps her visits short and tries to see her son elsewhere.

DIL thinks MIL wants to see too much of her son.

MIL is overprotective and overbearing with her son and this affects her relationship with DIL.

DIL thinks other MILs are less invested in their sons.

MIL is angry at her daughter and this affects her relationship with DIL, or she compares DIL unfavorably to her own daughter.

DIL is angry at her own mother and displaces this on MIL, or she compares MIL unfavorably to her own mother.

MIL thinks DIL has bad taste in clothes and household decoration and would like to help her to be more tasteful.

DIL dreads when MIL gives her gifts of clothes or items for the house because she dislikes MIL's taste. She uses gifts reluctantly and only when MIL visits.

MIL thinks DIL is disrespectful to offer advice to someone older and wiser and is defensive about her lifestyle.

DIL thinks MIL's lifestyle is unhealthy, outmoded, or stupid, and would like to help her change.

MIL thinks how awful it would be to be sick or frail and dependent on DIL, whose decisions or caretaking she doesn't trust.

DIL dreads that MIL might need help in old age, knowing that the task would fall on her, not MIL's son.

MIL wants her son to spend a good deal of time and attention on her and does not want equal time with DIL.

DIL is jealous of the attention her husband gives his mother, not her, and wishes MIL would give her the kinds of attention she gives her son.

MIL thinks DIL is a lousy cook, extravagant, or stingy.

DIL thinks MIL is a lousy cook, extravagant, or stingy. Neither wants to eat the other's cooking.

Here are some better scenarios:

MIL and DIL let go of expectations, criticism, resentment, blaming, displacement, and transfer.

They try to value each other and find good qualities.

They accept diverse backgrounds, different values, and generational differences and work at tolerance and acceptance.

They do not compete for the son/husband's attention or children/grandchildren's love; it is good for children to have many people who care for them.

Both realize that nobody is perfect.

MIL and DIL have interests outside of the relationship and enjoy friends, colleagues, neighbors, and other people.

Both MIL and DIL get satisfaction and recognition for paid or volunteer work or accomplishments.

Both save advice for people in a less loaded, problematic relationship than theirs.

Both realize the stresses each woman encounters in an ageist, sexist society and are supportive of each other.

Both listen with empathy to each other.

Both bite their tongues when necessary.

Both get support from others in the same boat.

Both get counseling if needed.

Both stop brooding. Neither thinks the son/husband's characteristics and behavior are the fault or property of the other, but the man in their lives is a human being with his own character, role, and decision-making process.

Reflections From the '70s

I am now the oldest person in my family – the matriarch. This gives me a lot of responsibility to be a good example of creative aging.

Longevity increased twenty-five years in the twentieth century, and the twenty-first century might bring even greater increases. So these days most of us are living longer than our parents or grandparents did. And, in living longer, we have to adapt to new roles and to infirmities. None of us want to be burdens on our adult children.

Therapists Joseph A. Ilardo, Ph.D., LCSW, and Carole R. Rothman, Ph.D., have written a book with a provocative title: *Are Your Parents Driving You Crazy? How to Resolve the Most Common Dilemmas with Aging Parents.*

Among the dilemmas they discuss are:
My father can no longer drive safely, but he refuses to surrender his license.
My mother is not poor, however, she scrimps to save money.
My eighty-two-year-old father wants to marry a woman he just met.
My mother can't manage her checking account any longer and she refuses my help.
My mother's frequent phone calls are just too much.

My mother is no longer stable on her feet and insists on climbing on a chair to reach the cabinets.

In all, the therapists discuss twenty-five difficulties between aging parents and their descendents and offer solutions and present problem-solving methods that can be applied to other aging parent situations. I read this book with interest and gave it to my daughter to read. Perhaps it will be helpful to you who have aging parents or are aging parents.

Another book I found useful is *Healthy Aging: Challenges and Solutions,* edited by Ken Dychtwald. Contributors are the nation's leading researchers, analysts, educators, physicians, gerontologists, and others, who write about the current crisis in health care and offer suggestions for changes that will help to ensure healthy aging. Though not light reading, this book helps us to be better informed. It is not a self-help book, but deals with policy and program issues. Editor Dychtwald has received the distinguished American Society on Aging award.

By 2030 nearly one quarter of the American population will be sixty-five or older. Marc Freedman has written *Prime Time: How Boomers Will Revolutionize Retirement and Transform America*. In this book, he introduces us to older adults who are making the most of the last third of their lives as volunteers and as vital members of their communities. We can all use role models, for today our lives are very different than for earlier generations. Freedman notes that the old concept of retirement as a year-long vacation is no longer viable. I agree.

Everywhere I go, I find other people who are doing exciting things, including helping others and pressing their creativity. However, at the same time we should not gloss over some of the real and difficult problems that come with aging. Here is a poem about a woman near eighty.

She drives fast and
often reads everything greedily,
indulges in television,
answers letters at length,
memorizes paintings,
favorite views, beloved faces,
necessary pathways, her front steps,
as her cataracts grow

It is true cataracts can be removed and knee and hip joint replacements and other remedies are brought to us by modern medicine. We can get hearing aids, physical therapy, and medications for various conditions. Yet living longer does not always mean optimum health. We owe it to ourselves and our descendents to follow a healthy lifestyle.

I resolve to keep educating myself about aging

and being a responsible elder. But I know things can happen and I know that while I adore old people who live outrageously and courageously, there are other people who are frail and need help and should get help. And that help is not always forthcoming in a society where the bottom line is money and where we are getting an increasingly mean, lean, and obscene medical care system.

The experts keep changing their advice, which makes it more and more confusing. Recently I went to a lecture on menopause. A prominent physician confessed that he had advised all of his older patients to walk to keep bones strong to prevent osteoporosis. Now, he says, we are advising that weight lifting may be more prudent.

Similarly, we have been told that certain foods were good – they are not, and that which we were advised not to eat may not have been so terrible after all.

So we read, go to lectures and discussion groups, network, use the computer, and attempt to seek accurate information for healthy aging. It is not easy.

Closer to eight than seventy, I wish myself luck and also wish good health to my readers – of all ages.

Since the alternative to aging is not good, we grope our way through the fog with hope and help from our loved ones and maybe from experts who change their advice.

In the end, we have to make our own decisions. And we have to strive for good relationships with our adult children, who I prefer to call descendants. We have to keep a balance between taking their advice and maintaining our autonomy. And they have to respect our autonomy and when and how to give advice.

Best wishes, folks. Happy Birthdays.

Journaling

24/7 Therapy

Your Dr. Ruth recommends that readers buy themselves journals. They can be fancy cloth-covered journals of the sort available in gift shops or stationary stores, or large, cheap notebooks. The reason I suggest journals is that you can write in them some of the things that are best left unsaid to others and some of the things that will preserve memories and make sense of your life.

Journaling is venting, catharsis, creative expression, reminiscence, and a jumping-off place for the rest of your life. Some people write in their journals daily and some when they feel the need, which could be often or infrequently. You can write for a few minutes or as long as you want or need.

Frankly, I decided to write on the topic of journaling because of a woman I encounter almost daily who insists on telling me things about her life that I am not really interested in and don't have the time to hear. I am always kind and polite and listen to this woman who needs to talk. However, I think she may be driving other people away from her and might unload the trivial, self-centered stuff onto journal pages and not bore people. In writing, she might discover also that she needs more stimulation in her life and be involved in outside activities. In writing, we experience self-discovery.

Unless we want to share or publish it, our journal lets us record our most private thoughts. Also it is cheaper than seeing a therapist and journals are available daily, twenty-four hours. People who keep journals often learn a lot and experience growth by reading over their journals. I know a woman who reads a year's jottings on New Year's Day and it is a revelation to her of how she spent her year and how she might want to change things in the next year.

May Sarton, Elizabeth Vining and many others published their journals, and some of my readers might publish theirs or parts thereof. Journals are often treasured family heirlooms telling about the lives of ancestors. However, if you don't want anyone to read your journal, you can always write on the first page, "To be destroyed in case of my demise."

How do you write a journal? The short answer is any way you want. Certainly, you can take journal writing workshops or get books from the library or a bookstore on writing that will serve as guidelines, but here are some suggestions:

If you want to write daily, you might make a set time for doing so. One woman wakes up, has coffee, then writes in her journal early so there will be no phone interruptions. She feels freshest and most perceptive then. One man writes a record of his day and thoughts at night in bed. He keeps the journal on his night table in case he wakes up in the middle of the night and wants to add to it some insight given him by a dream.

Don't censor yourself. Write freely and don't worry about spelling, sentence structure, punctuation, and so forth. If you just keep writing, you may be surprised at what comes up. You may start with something trivial that will lead to something important.

Of course, you can keep a journal on your computer if you wish, rather than in handwritten form. Be sure to print a hard copy so you won't lose your valuable thoughts. And don't write your journal on odd little scraps of paper around the house as you will most likely lose track of them and deprive yourself of the pleasure and insight of reading in the future.

The truth is that none of us have a perfect memory. If you write down your ideas and feelings, and record events in your life, you will always have evidence to trigger your memory. In fact, writing or any creative activity helps improve our memory skills and brain growth and may ward off such nasty diseases as Alzheimer's.

You can use your journal to put down the pros and cons of a decision you must make and explore the alternatives.

You can take your journal along on a trip and

record interesting scenery and happenings, or describe the people you meet. This will help you re-live your travels and also share them accurately with others. Try to capture the details that you might otherwise forget.

You can use your journal to record your anger at people who have annoyed you. You can journal an unsent letter to them and that way get your anger onto the paper and off your chest and yet maintain the relationships.

You can use your journal as a gold mine of things you may later refine for lectures or for publication. I often jot down things in my journals that I later turn into poems or articles.

When you think you have nothing to write, start doodling in your journal. Perhaps your subconscious will be awakened. Drawing, even if you don't consider yourself an artist, can prime the pump.

Topics you might consider writing about:
• What I like (dislike) about myself.
• What I like (dislike) about a certain person.
• Things I am grateful for.
• Things I am afraid of.
• Things I wish for.
• Ways I have changed.
• If I were a color (or an animal), what I would be.
• What spring (summer, fall, winter) means to me.

- How do I feel about my age?
- What does Christmas or any holiday mean to me?
- What do I remember about a holiday past?
- How I am creative.
- How I have grown recently.
- If I only had one year to live, what would I do with it?
- What do I want with the rest of my life?
- What I did when I was six (or any childhood age).
- Write a letter to some part of your body.
- My favorite teacher was and why.
- What I love (despise).
- What I would do if I won the lottery.
- The best advice I could give a young person today.
- What I remember about my grandparents.
- Ten achievements in my life.
- Ten societal changes in my lifetime.
- Aging is ___, or my body is ___, or friendship is ___, or love is ___, and so forth

Enjoy your journaling. It may surprise you.

Some Resolutions
for Older People

What follow are some resolutions which you
might want to try:

- Carrot cake will not count as one of my
  required daily vegetables.
- I will satisfy my chocolate craving by making
  skim milk mildly chocolate milkshakes instead of
  eating candy, ice cream, cake, or brownies. That
  way I will get a dose of calcium from the milk as
  I "chocolatize." (I may cheat on this one.)
- I will not watch television in bed at night
  because I will fall asleep, be awakened an hour
  later by a loud commercial, and then be restless
  because I do not easily fall back to sleep.
- I will stop buying new clothes until I have given
  away or thrown away the clutter in my closet.
  You know, the clothes hanging there until I lose
  weight, come back in style, or stop being wrinkled because I refuse to iron.
- I will immediately throw away mail that I think I
  might read later and never do, eliminating
  messy, guilt-engendering piles.
- I will stop subscribing to magazines that I
  ought to read and subscribe to those that I
  really will read. I will follow this practice also
  when signing out library books.
- I will stop buying things that I might use as gifts

someday. It is a nuisance to find places to store the stuff and I also might forget I have them.

- I will stop worrying that I can't remember the names of everyone I have met and realize that I have met so many nice people, including former students, that it is impossible to remember all their names.

- I now have a nice suitcase with wheels. I will throw out those no-wheelers and in the process go through my home and toss things I have been hoarding for no apparent reason.

- I will stop taking things home from the take-and-leave place at the dump. But if you see me taking something irresistible, please look the other way.

- I will say "no" to people when I really don't want to do what they ask. This will be hard. Like most women, I was raised to be a pleaser and to always put others first.

- I will shorten or dispose of my floor-length skirts and dresses because I have "shrunk." My clothes are hazardous and I could trip over longer hemlines.

- Despite the cost of heating fuel I will not risk hypothermia by staying in a cold house. I will remind other frugal elders that hypothermia may be irreversible and life-threatening.

- Although you can't tell from this list, I will bite my tongue when I want to give advice to those who are not asking. I will remember that I have two ears for listening and but one mouth.

- Since, at our ages, we probably should not even buy green bananas, I will not postpone doing things I really want to do and will wear my best clothes all the time instead of saving them for a special occasion.
- I will stop agonizing and apologizing for the things I did wrong in life and start praising for that which I did correctly.
- I will stop wearing black because I think it makes me look thinner. I'm going to wear the bright color I enjoy.
- I will not pay for and will use without guilt address labels sent to me by worthy or unworthy causes in which I have no interest.
- I will start giving to unorganized, disorganized charity – not organized charities with highly paid executives and disproportionate administrative costs.
- I will feed the squirrels. Sample at store salad bars. Write radical graffiti.
- I will scold strangers honking car horns and parking in disabled spots and those who talk on the phone while driving.
- I will break the tree-wasting Christmas card chain by not responding and returning a card to people I knew so long ago. I really don't care to greet them.
- I will walk out of boring events, dry speeches, and dull movies even if a few people have to move so I can squeeze by.

Illness

Recommendations When You or Others Are Ill

Dr. Ruth has some recommendations for dealing with your own illness or responding to the illness of others. Some of the advice is from personal experience when I had surgery three years ago. So you might prepare in case an emergency occurs.

Make a list of people with their telephone numbers you might want to call from the hospital, even if you think you know these numbers. You may be groggy from medication and not remember these numbers. Many hospitals provide bedside telephones. You can call local numbers free but hospitals do not supply telephone directories. Also, since it costs to call information, hospital telephones are often programmed so that you cannot call information, only free local calls.

Give a photocopy of this list to your spouse, close friend, or adult children, marking the names of people who have offered to help in some way. Your son or daughter, spouse, or helping friend can then use this list to inform people of your progress or ask for help. Because of HIPAA regulations, hospitals do not give progress reports on patients, but may put calls through to patients' rooms. If you are recovering from surgery or otherwise ill, you may find it a burden to answer a lot of phone calls and may prefer someone else to be an informant on your condition. Also, don't hesitate to turn the phone off altogether if talking is a burden. Your job is to get well, not to give bulletins. Many people who call want more details than you have the energy to give. Don't be afraid to cut people off by saying "I'm tired."

Take a good-sized notebook to the hospital. If you take a tiny one it may fall and get lost or not be big enough. This notebook is useful to write down the names of the many doctors who may visit you, and allows you to write down their instructions. You can also jot down lists of things you want to ask the doctors or family when they visit and their replies.

I found my notebook invaluable when I was in the hospital and when I got home. Also, bring more than one pen or pencil because they tend to roll off of the bedside table or get borrowed.

If you are a decaffeinated herb tea drinker, bring your own stock. Most hospitals have decaffeinated coffee and tea but not herb tea. I don't like to take sleeping meds, but do find that two Celestial Seasonings Sleepytime tea bags brewed to a strong cup can put me to sleep, especially when I wake up at night. To solve the brewing problem, my wonderful daughter brewed up strong Sleepytime tea and put it in a large soda bottle by my bedside. When I woke up at night I could open and drink it at room temperature, and it did its job.

If you have some other favorite non-perishable food or vitamin, take it to the hospital with you.

Realize that most hospitals are overheated compared to our homes. Take light clothes if you do not plan to wear hospital Johnnies. The beds are hot because they have plastic over the mattresses and pillows.

When hospitalized, do not be afraid to tell visitors when you are exhausted and want them to go. In fact, I asked people not to send flowers because semiprivate rooms have little space for flowers.

When you are in the hospital, do not be afraid to ask for a room change if you have an impossible roommate. Sometimes a room change will not be possible, but it is worth trying. I had one roommate who was deranged and screamed all night. The nurses were very understanding about my room as it was close to midnight and I could not get to sleep.

When you do go home, do not hesitate to ask for help from friends and neighbors. They feel good about helping. I kept a list of chores that needed to be done and asked each visitor to do one or two. For instance, I asked one to do a load of wash since I could not use the stairs to get to it. I asked several visitors to help me put on elastic stockings. I asked a number of visitors to get my mail or to mail my letters for me. My neighbors went shopping for me and took my trash to the landfill.

Don't worry about returning the kindness people extend to you. You would do the same for them or do for others in the cycle of giving and receiving. Sometimes it is better to give than receive.

People will bring you cooked food, so if you suspect they are going to bring food, tell them you have a special diet. Mine is low sodium and I asked that salt not be used.

One of the things I found delightful while recovering is that my friend Doty Waring brought me lunch and enough for herself so we had companionship. So did my friend Ellie Mamber. Two members of my Quaker meeting, Char White and Susan McGarvey called and said they were bringing dinner and we would eat together. The dinner was so ample that I had leftovers for the next day.

Also, several friends transported me back and forth to the hospital for tests and follow-up visits. I appreciated this much more than I would have appreciated flowers. So line up your network for needed services which they will be glad to give. And if you don't have enough friends, work on making more as they are good insurance.

If you live alone and will be weak or at risk, you may want to order *Lifeline*, which is an emergency response system. I have it, and after my discharge from the hospital I felt comfortable that any hour of the day or night from anywhere in my house, I could hit a button from my wrist or around my neck and get immediate help. *Lifeline* can be found at 1-800-451-0525.

Also, I have a few guidelines for people who want to help the ill.

- Sick people may need to vent their anger and difficulties, so listen patiently. Don't push people to talk and give more details than their energy or inclination permits.
- Telling ill people your own medical difficulties or the difficulties of others does not help them to count their blessings or feel they are better off than others. Refrain from this.
- Don't waste your money on expensive get-well cards. A short note is just as much appreciated. My friend Helen Hicks sent me amusing or interesting enclosures cut from the paper, or copies from other sources.

I hope you and your friends and relatives all stay well, but if there is an illness, perhaps this will prove useful. Best wishes for good health.

An Open Letter to Doctors

An open letter to my now and future doctors may interest you and you might even want to share it with your own doctor or write one of your own.

Dear Doctor,

I need to tell you how I want to be treated as I age. Like other Americans, doctors are not immune from ageism and the stereotypes about the old. I am grateful for your knowledge that can help me age well but want you to keep in mind the points I list below. Perhaps my list will be useful with other patients and you might even share it with your staff and colleagues.

1. Do not treat me as stupid because I am old. Intelligence does not decline with age, contrary to stereotypes.
2. You may call me by my first name, but many older patients, brought up in an era of different etiquette, prefer to be addressed as Mr., Mrs., or Miss with their last name. Of course, if you want me to call you by your first name, that alters the etiquette.
3. Do not assume you can bypass old people in your waiting room to take care of younger patients because the old people's time is less valuable.
4. Do not overmedicate me. Some physicians do

not realize medications are retained longer in the systems of old people and old people have more adverse reactions to medications.

5. On the other hand, do not refrain from giving me needed medication because you think everything wrong with me is just old age.

6. Please write out prescriptions clearly so that my pharmacist won't make an error and so I can do some research on the medication.

7. If I ask for help for depression or seem depressed, take it seriously. Take the time to see if there is a physiological basis for the depression, as there often is in older people. If you carefully rule out physical causes, do not attribute my depression to my age. Do not assume that I am too old for therapy or lifestyle change. Make the proper suggestions or referral. Too many physicians load elders up with psychotropic medications which might not be needed and which can be addictive and make people groggy. Anti-depressant medication can be valuable but it needs to be given carefully, after full investigation, not casually.

8. Should I ask for sleeping pills, I hope you will remember that many old people fall and hurt themselves when foggy. Explore what is contributing to my sleeplessness and what lifestyle changes could help. Maybe, like many old people, I will forget that we need less sleep as we age, not more, and that daytime naps cut down

on the amount of night sleep.

9. If I come to your office with a relative or friend, do not question and talk to that person instead of me. Many of my friends cannot drive and when their daughters take them to doctors, the doctors assume the elders incompetent and ask the daughters the questions and give her the information. One woman I know who took her daughter to help her remember the doctor's instructions was humiliated when the doctor asked the daughter, "How often does she move her bowels?" The woman replied, "Don't ask my daughter – I'm sitting right here."

10. If I become hard of hearing, please be patient and don't scream at me. When you scream it is very unpleasant.

11. Please do not ignore my questions. I will try to be brief and come in with a written list. These questions are important to me and I deserve answers or at least a statement that you don't know.

12. Allocate enough time for our visits. I know you need to earn money, but please do not allow so little time per visit that I go away frustrated and angry.

13. Be honest with me. Too many doctors treat old patients like children who cannot handle the truth. I want the diagnosis and prognosis. I can handle it.

14. If you can't help me, refer me to someone who

can. Also, please do not assume I am worthless at my age and should not have the best treatment available. Do not cut health costs at my expense. Argue with insurers if necessary. I deserve a quality life.

15. However, if I am suffering terribly from a fatal disease and there is no hope, do not let me suffer by undermedicating me or using extreme measures to keep me breathing.

16. If you have women or elders in your life who you do not like, please do not displace those negative feelings onto me. I am not your mother, your grandmother, or your ex-wife. I am me, a person who needs your best thought and compassion. Life is not easy for the old. Don't make it any harder than it is.

Well reader, that is the end of my letter.

Antideterioration and Sleep Suggestions

Everywhere there are articles and pamphlets with the danger signs of diseases. Taking a leaf from this, your Dr. Ruth wants to give you a list of warning signs of deterioration. Nobody is perfect, but if you have too many of these signs, you'd better consider changing your lifestyle somewhat.

I think you are deteriorating when:

- The first thing you do each morning is to consult the paper or TV guide to see what is on TV that day.
- Your chief topic of conversation is reports on your worries, illness, or pains and the worries, illness, and pains of others.
- You read the obituaries before you read the news.
- You stop doing new things.
- You stop going to new places.
- You stop trying new foods.
- You stop trying to make new friends.
- You stop reading new authors.
- You spend a lot of time complaining about young people these days, their activities, values, clothing, music, and so forth.

- You deny your need for bifocal glasses or a hearing aid.
- You lie about your age because you are ashamed of aging or have not come to terms with it.
- You lose interest in your appearance.
- You can afford to buy new clothes but don't because "who cares?"
- You never use your good dishes but only use a few you keep in your sink or drainer.
- You respond to any suggestion that anyone makes with the words "yes but."
- You procrastinate so long about answering letters that you feel guilty and begin to hate the friend or relative to whom you should be writing.
- You are unable to throw anything away including what you don't use and never will use.
- You avoid all exercise, even gentle exercise like walking or sitting down exercises.

Is there some reason, like low thyroid, anemia, or reactions to medication that is making you lethargic? Or maybe you need some counseling on how to have a happy, productive old age. If you only do a few of the things listed above, well okay. But, if a lot of them describe you, consider whether you are in a rut and how to get out of it. At our ages, it is a shame not to enjoy life. We worked hard raising families and in jobs and this ought to be a good time for us. I know it is hard if you are short of money, but there are a lot of free services and events available to us seasoned citizens. I also know it is difficult if you can't get good medical attention or transportation, but we can have a good time advocating for those services. Speaking your mind to officials and the press can be an antidote to passivity and being stuck with anger. In fact, unexpressed anger can lead to being in a funk.

Sometimes people do not have a desire to do things because they are having sleep difficulties. One of the most common complaints of older people and people generally is that they are not getting sufficient quality sleep. One study of nine thousand elders living independently, not in insti-tutions, showed that 50 percent of them com-plained about not sleeping well. Actually, another study of American adults of all ages revealed that one third reported sleep difficulties. Complaints from both studies included taking a long time to fall asleep, more awakenings, pains from arthritis and other diseases disturbing sleep, restless legs, having to get up to go to the bathroom, etc.

The truth is that it is normal for older people to wake up often during the night and have fewer periods of REM sleep (very deep sleep). Also, many elders find they awake in the morning earlier than they would like. Sometimes the medications we take create sleeping difficulties. Taking medica-

161

tions to sleep is usually not a good idea because they can make us groggy and cause falls when we get up.

Exercise during the day can help our sleep. Also, a regular bedtime and limiting daytime naps can help. Some people find milk or a light snack at bedtime helpful. I find that setting my clock radio with an automatic shut off for an hour helps me fall asleep. Pleasant thoughts or soothing visualizations at bedtime can help. Avoid bedtime brooding about tasks you must do, your troubles, and the troubles of your loved ones.

Since it is normal to wake at night, some of us elders have ways of filling the time until we get to sleep again. I happen to love news and enjoy listening to it when I am awake in the middle of the night or early morning. Other people have favorite talk or music shows they like, or keep a book bedside to nod off on. Obviously, a peaceful book rather than a scary or exciting book is indicated.

Heavy drapes or dark shades can keep early morning light from wakening us. However, people vary in their sleep patterns. There are owls who like the nighttime and larks who like the early morning.

Some people are awakened by vivid dreams and like to write them in a notebook kept by their beds. It is natural to dream of events and people in our past, but if nightmares constantly disturb us, we might want to talk to a therapist. Certainly, if we can't get sufficient sleep, we might want to consult a physician to see if there are physical and medical situations in our lives that cause this and changes that can be made to improve sleep.

Several important sleep studies are now being conducted throughout the country and the future may bring some advice on sleeping. Meanwhile, experts suggest good sleep hygiene, which means regular time to sleep and not spending time in bed trying to sleep when sleep doesn't come, so that we begin to hate the thought of bedtime. We may need to stay up later watching television or doing something else until we are ready for sleep.

I hope your sleep is good and your dreams are happy ones. Don't worry if you don't get as much sleep as you did at one time in your life. Adolescents can sleep long times often. But if we sleep less well in later life, we are consistent with our peers.

New Things To Do

It is time to do something new. For seasoned citizens, it is especially important to do novel things because this can be stimulating and make the dendrites in our brains grow to prevent senility.

What we choose to do will vary with our taste and circumstances, but it is important not to stay in a rut, comfortable though that may seem. Even though we have had long lives and done much, there are different things to try that may promote growth and enrich our lives, besides helping our brain cells.

Here are some suggestions for new things you might do, though hopefully, you will have lots of ideas of your own.

- Since America is becoming very diverse, you might learn a few words in the language of some of our newer immigrants such as some Spanish words, Portuguese words, Korean words, and so forth. You could also go to the library and read up on the cultural heritage of new Americans.
- Attend one service at a house of worship other than your own. This will give you a knowledge of other's religions.
- Read in a genre that is new to you. If you have always taken fiction out of the library, go to the

nonfiction or poetry section and explore. If you have never read mysteries, try reading a mystery book. If you think feminism is terrible, try reading a feminist book you got out of the women's section at the bookstore. You might be surprised that feminism is different from what you thought. If you have thought plays were only to see at a theater, try getting some plays out of the library and reading them aloud with your friends or alone.

- Take a walk where you have never walked before. Instead of a familiar walk in your own neighborhood, take a different route, or drive your car someplace else, park it, then take a walk in that area. Or if you are a winter mall walker, when weather is bad outside, go to a different mall to walk.
- Take a course at a college.
- Do a different kind of volunteer work than you have done before.
- Try a new food even if you think you may not like it. Many people who turned up their noses at Tofu or other relatively unfamiliar products have discovered new taste sensations and new healthy and economical eating. Try new recipes or alter old ones.
- Change your way of dressing. If you have always been conservative in your clothes, try becoming flamboyant. Wear a color you've never worn.

- Get a new hairstyle. I know an older woman who had worn her hair for years long with a bun on top of her head. She got her hair cut stylishly short and took to wearing dramatic earrings. She and her friends loved the change.
- If you can afford it, take a trip to the kind of place you have never gone before. Talk to the locals, overcoming your shyness.
- If you have never kept a journal, start now.
- If you have never bought yourself fresh flowers in the winter, buy some.
- Telephone somebody you have never called before. Perhaps this is a person you met briefly once.
- Go to a different kind of movie than you usually see. If you hate it and it is a theater with multiple movies, you can always sneak down the corridor and slip into another movie. But you might find that it is interesting to see a different kind of film than is your habit.
- If you have not been a bird watcher, buy a bird book and binoculars and become one.
- Get the kind of pet you have never had before. Visit a pet store for ideas.
- Change around the decorations in your home, or if you can afford it, opt for a new color scheme by buying some new things. If you have been subdued, go for bright colors. And while you are at it, put larger watt bulbs in your lamps and overhead lights. As we age, we need

more light and too many of us economize on light and get sleepy or even worse, fall. I no longer stand on chairs to change high bulbs. I ask a young neighbor or wait until one of my descendents come to visit or I have some other younger visitors. I suggest you do the same.

- Visit a neighbor you have never visited before. You might find a new friend. You could bring an offering of some baked goods or a few flowers and say you'd like to get to know the neighbor. If you get rebuffed, you will survive.
- Learn how to play the musical instrument you have always enjoyed hearing. Take some lessons or get an instruction book.
- If you have never written a letter to the editor or a politician, do so now. You might do some good and get something off your chest.
- Shop in a different store instead of the familiar one.
- Get a flower or tree book from the library or bookstore and learn the names of trees and flowers. Then, on your spring and summer walks, you can identify these and impress anyone you are walking with.
- Learn a game you have never played. This could be a game that provides physical exercise or one that provides mental stimulation. If you have never played card games, you can learn them.
- Try drawing or painting, even if you haven't

done so since the sixth grade. Or try a craft.

- Try memorizing some poems, jokes or other interesting things you can share with others.
- Try doing something you have always considered the domain of the other gender. If you are a woman who thought only men could know about cars, study up on cars and learn to do simple or more complex things to your car. I learned recently that I could put in my own windshield wiper fluid and oil, and put air in my tires. If you are a man, you could learn to sew, knit, cook, or clean if you have never done these things before. These are only for instances. There are many things we have never done as males or females because we were brought up in an era when activities were more gender separated than today.

Make your own list of new things you will try, and best wishes growing and expanding your life and brain. Be an OPAL, which is an Old Person Actively Living.

Bereavement, Loneliness, and the Holidays

This is for the recently bereaved, people who live alone, and those who love them. One of my readers wrote me how hard it was to face the holiday season without her dear deceased sister with whom she had lived lifelong and with whom she had celebrated the holidays.

In addition to their religious significance, the December holidays and New Year's are important to people and the sociability function of the holidays is often very painful to people who feel left out, such as widows, widowers, the divorced, and other singles. Seasoned citizens whose families are at a distance or who have no families may feel especially lonely because everyone else seems to be involved in communal festivities.

Actually, more people are alone at holiday seasons than alone persons realize. So the first suggestion is not to assume that you are the only one who has nothing to do on the holidays. Reach out to other people. You may find they will be very grateful if you suggest sharing a meal, shopping, a movie, a concert, or just visiting. One widow I know put a notice up on the bulletin board at her housing complex inviting people to come share a potluck meal in the community room on Christmas. Eleven grateful people were happy she took the initiative and they had a splendid shared meal and a good time together.

Also, do not be too proud or elitist. Go to the community events that are arranged for people who are alone. Call your local Council on Aging and check your local newspaper and houses of worship to see what is going on that you can attend. You may even meet new friends that way.

Particularly painful to many bereaved is remembering the happy holidays shared with those who have died. Do not think that you should suppress such memories of this person at the holiday events. This person was part of your life and bringing up the memories and the person may bring a tear, but tears are not bad. They can be therapeutic by releasing instead of internalizing your grief. Shared tears bring families together and strengthen them. We also can celebrate the life and special characteristics of the person who died. This can help keep this person alive for us.

A woman in one of my workshops told me how one Christmas her widowed mother sat at the head of the table the year after her husband died. The whole family, sons, daughters, and grandchildren, were sad because the father/grandfather was gone. The widow offered grace at the beginning of the meal and mentioned in it how they missed Dad, but them she cursed him for taking his wonderful secret stuffing recipe with him to his grave. Everyone's tears turned to laughter and the tension was broken. It is good to reminisce.

I spent one Fourth of July on an island in Maine where my friends had summered for years. At the annual Fourth of July lobster fest, people missed Bill, who was very beloved and now dead. What we all did was tell Bill stories of the funny things he had said and the wonderful things he did. I think this was much better for his widow that we acknowledged his life as part of the community rather than ignoring that he had been among us and enriched us.

It also helps when we are alone to write out our feelings. Don't worry about style, spelling, or grammar. Just put down on paper how you are feeling. You may find that it helps to get it outside of you. Some people have written unsent letters to a lost loved one as a sort of way of communicating.

Of course, talking to a good friend, neighbor, or relative about your feelings can also be helpful. If you are really depressed, you should seek professional help from a physician, social worker, or counselor. Your local Council on Aging director or hospital can refer you to someone who can help you deal with severe holiday blues. There are also groups in most communities for the bereaved. It can help to be with other people who are working through the same issues.

Some people have found that a change of scene helps over the holidays and they plan to attend an Elderhostel, Senior Venture program, or go visit a friend or relative in another part of the country.

One way to handle the holidays if you are feeling deprived is to reach out to those who are even worse off. Then you feel good because you are helping. Some people go to nursing homes on the holidays to visit those who have no visitors and bring little gifts. Others reach out to children who would not otherwise have much holiday cheer. People in religious congregations, for example, bring gifts and foods to the homeless families housed in dreary motel rooms by the state. There are many needy people who can benefit by your giving of yourself. When I lost a child through death, I was helped most by volunteering at the Veteran's Hospital. I felt needed, and in helping, I was healed somewhat.

If you cannot afford to go away, can you plan some pleasant local activities? Some people use pretty indoor shopping malls as parks in the winter, taking their daily walks there and then sitting and watching people go by.

Can you sign up for a course free or nearly free to seasoned citizens at a local college or in an adult education program in your town? Can you start writing your autobiography, develop a new hobby, join a new organization, volunteer?

Just having a library hour or two a day where you get dressed and read the magazines, papers, and books may help. Libraries are usually cheerful, warm, and cozy in the winter. You might meet some new people there. Ask someone out for coffee. Check the bulletin board to see what is going on in town while you are at the library. You may be surprised at all there is to do. Some libraries even show movies once a week.

Beating Summer Heat

We seasoned citizens long for summer during the icy, cold winter. However, summer can be difficult if there is a hot spell. Our human thermostats are not as efficient as we age so the heat may bother us terribly.

When we were children we could be cooled down and happy with the two- or three-cent cups of sherbert we could buy in the 1930s Depression days. Now some of us have air conditioners and fans to make the hot weather tolerable.

However, not all seasoned citizens can afford air conditioning and fans, and some who can afford them do not like being isolated in our houses during hot weather.

Your Dr. Ruth has some suggestions for staying comfortable during the hot weather.

- Keep your shades and blinds down and drawn to block the hot sunlight. Air out the residence at night and in the early morning before the sun is high.
- Spend time in air conditioned public places. Many libraries are now air conditioned and you can spend comfortable hours there reading papers, magazines, and books. If the library in your own city or town is not air conditioned, call around to find a library in a nearby city or town that is air conditioned. You are entitled to

use libraries in municipalities other than the one in which you reside. By going to cool libraries, you will also save money on newspapers, magazines, and books. Some libraries even have video machines.

- Many seasoned citizens use shopping malls as cool places to walk and sit in the summer. If you go with a friend or friends, you can have a nice chat. If you go alone, you can people watch. Of course, there is always the danger that you might be seduced by the merchandise displays and buy more than you can afford. If so, leave your checks, charge cards, and most of your cash at home. Summers are great times for sales in malls. Many seasoned citizens combine two things – cooling off in the summer and buying Christmas and Chanukah presents early at the sales.

- Many seasoned citizens need to watch our calorie and fat intake so should not be constantly eating ice cream or even low-fat frozen yogurt. A nice way to make yourself treats is to pour your favorite juice into your ice cube tray. You then have delicious squares as a frozen treat. Some people put wooden or plastic sticks in each cube section so they can suck on cube coolers like we used to do on popsicles. You can, of course, use no sugar beverages to freeze for minimum calories. Another great hot day treat is to freeze grapes and suck on them one at a time until they thaw sufficiently to chew them. Delicious and relatively low calorie and good for you.

- Many lakes in state parks have low or free senior citizen rates and there are public swimming pools in many areas. Check with your local recreation department to see what might be available.
- Some seasoned citizens I know house-sit in the summer for people who have pools or air-conditioned houses, but still go away on vacation. By caring for their houses, pets, and plants, you can get a vacation of your own in a nice place. Try asking around and putting ads in newspapers for this. Notices of your availability can also be put up on church or temple bulletin boards and other such places.
- Some seasoned citizens who live in the city choose the hot summer to go to Elderhostels that are in the country. You can get an Elderhostel catalog at your senior center, public library, or from Elderhostel. Elders may also stay at American Youth Hostels which do not provide programs like Elderhostels, but do give you an inexpensive place to stay.
- Besides heat, another summer hazard for seasoned citizens is sun. Sun can give us skin cancers or macular degeneration, an eye disease which can lead to loss of vision. So it is very important to wear a wide-brimmed hat and

sunglasses when in the sun and to cover bare skin with light clothing or use sun block. Try to be in the sun only early in the morning and very late in the day.

- Synthetic fabrics tend to make us hotter than cotton clothes, so if possible, wear light cotton clothes during hot days.
- If you are outrageous like your Dr. Ruth, you can also hang out in nice air-conditioned hotel lobbies. These have comfortable chairs. You can people watch or read the newspaper as if waiting for someone. Ones where airport limos pick up people are good because they will think you are waiting for an airport limo. Or you can act as if you are waiting for a friend to join you to lunch in the hotel's restaurant. But don't fall asleep and snore.
- I even know people who hang out in air-conditioned hospital lobbies during the hot weather. Hey, it is better than going to the hospital for heat prostration.

Changing Rules

As seasoned citizens, we are thankful for many things. However, one of the things that enrages us as we age is that they keep changing the rules. What was once considered good is now bad. We were brought up in a time when eggs, butter, whole milk and roast beef were considered terrific foods. Our mothers fed us custards with eggs and milk. Baked goods were a sign of love, not of cholesterol danger. We fed our own children according to the food charts then. Now things have changed and foods we were taught were good are now on the bad list.

Also, when we were young and our children were young, it was thought that being outdoors in the sun was good for you. We made sure our children got to the beach and other places where they could benefit from the sun's rays. Things have changed dramatically. We who loved the sun have to divorce ourselves from it because of the shrinking ozone layer and new medical dictums.

The sun has become evil
an enemy, anathema
causing skin cancers
macular eye degeneration
days of dangerous heat
beyond deodorants and coping

dehydration, dried up gardens,
glare for dangerous driving.

We who loved the sun
turn from it in horror
welcome cloudy days
shady spots, rain
sunset, nighttime
even grayness.
Nothing is hated more
than a former lover
who betrayed.

Then there is the issue of weight. We were taught that a plump baby and child was a healthy baby and child. Then the experts decided that thin was in. Now, they are revising again, saying not too thin, especially for older people. They keep changing the weight charts on us and we are supposed to change our bodies accordingly.

Fashion, of course, is another gripe. Just when we finally get around to throwing out old but good clothes because they are out of style, the style comes back. In fact, some of the clothes we threw out in innocence have now become collectors' items and are sold in Vintage Clothing stores for big money we could use if we hadn't disposed of them earlier. The same is true for furniture. Many of us modernized our rooms in a time when old furniture was disdained. Now the furniture we dumped is back in.

Then there are those of us who, to prevent fires and vermin, cleaned out all the comic books our children left when they flew the nest. Those old comic books are now worth substantial money. Our children have not forgiven us for throwing them away. It makes you afraid to throw anything away, but then they accuse you of being senile because you are living in clutter.

Another rule that has changed regards exercise. When we were young, old people were allowed to rest and relax as the reward for a lifetime of work. Now, we are told that even a daily walk is not enough. We are supposed to take out a membership in a health club and learn how to lift weights and run elaborate exercise machinery. If we don't, we are warned of dire consequences. We are told to get out of the rocking chair, stop being couch potatoes and sweat and groan our way to longevity.

Then there is the backlash against having a nice retirement. In more prosperous times, people accepted that elders could finally enjoy travel and recreation and live in nice retirement facilities that we had worked hard to earn. Now, in a time of recession, struggling midlifers and young people resent us if we seem to lead an easy leisure life. And if we need medical care or long-term care, they call us societal burdens. This certainly doesn't seem fair after all we gave to our families, at the workplace, and to our communities.

Also, it is hard for us who grew up in less environmentally aware times to adapt to the new rules. At one time, a green lawn and nice garden were marks of a good neighbor. Now, we are not supposed to use scarce water even if we can afford the skyrocketing costs. Once, we burned or put out our trash or took it to the dump. In our old age we have to learn recycling.

Also, language changes. Just as we figure out and begin to use the new expressions of younger generations, they change the expressions. We try to stay current in our language, but they snicker at us. We have to get used to using Ms. instead of Miss or Mrs. And to change our language to eliminate gender bias. Mailmen must now be called mail carriers and repairman becomes repair person, for example. We may have called our women friends "girls" but that is no longer acceptable.

Of course tax rules change constantly and the music we liked all our lives is harder to get on the radio. Manners we thought were important are now considered unnecessary or quaint.

Driving at reasonable speeds we are used to gets us honked at by rude people who drive by in powerful new cars. People think us archaic because we use typewriters or pen instead of computers and because we write letters instead of making long distance calls. Furniture now has to be assembled. Card catalogues we used to love in libraries have been replaced by computers we hate. Folks think us obsolete if we don't have answering machines or faxes, even though we had full lives without them.

Perhaps worst of all, clergy and physicians who we had thought of as utterly trustworthy now turn out, in some instances, to be unethical, sexually exploitive, and to have other grave faults. We wonder who you can trust.

Moving Your Home

Moving is generally difficult at any age. To move when we are old involves special difficulties. Surveys have shown that most people prefer to age in place, in their accustomed surroundings with the accumulated possessions of a lifetime. However, often late in life it becomes necessary to move. It may be burdensome or even impossible to maintain a house and that house may now be too large for us. Snow and leaf removal and ground maintenance and housekeeping may become difficult or impossible. Some of us hire people to do various chores for us. But it is not always easy to get the proper help. Our possessions may become nuisances because of the care they require and the clutter. We may no longer be able to drive and there may be no public transportation.

Additionally, we may be lonely and feel isolated. If we have lost a spouse, we may want the companionship possible in a retirement community, but even couples often want activities that are organized for them. Also, some people as they age require services such as meals, transportation, help with medications, bathing, etc.

There is now a sometimes bewildering variety of alternatives available. There are continuing care retirement communities which offer independent living in apartments and some services including one meal or more per day. These places also usu-ally provide assisted living with more services when needed and a nursing home component. Then there are places that have only independent living, so if you require assisted living or a nursing home, you must go elsewhere to bring in services. Of course, there is a big price differential. Waiting lists are often long at good inexpensive places.

Some places are non-profit and some are profit-making. Some are very pricey and some are less so. Certain cities and towns have subsidized affordable elderly housing. A few cities and towns also include market value units. And some organi-zations or private developers mix subsidized housing with market value housing. You need to investigate places you are interested in to find out. Some places have large entrance fees and monthly fees and others just rent.

It is very important first to ask yourself a lot of questions. Just what are your needs and what ser-vices and location do you want? What can you afford? Add up what you pay now for utilities, taxes, upkeep, mortgage if any, etc., and compare this with the cost of the new place.

Then you need to ask a lot of questions about the places you are considering. You must be care-ful to read all of the fine print, visit extensively, and inquire about the financial integrity and sta-bility of the developer, owner or organization. Some places ask you for a deposit before a place is built or a deposit to be on a waiting list. Make sure you will get this back if you change your mind or the project is not built.

I put down $1,000 to be on a priority list for a retirement village in the planning stage. There was a non-profit institution in the forefront but a commercial development company involved. People were assured they would get the $1,000 back if we decided not to proceed to the next stage of putting down a substantial amount of money. I decided not to go ahead and asked for my $1,000 back. I was told I would have to wait two weeks. That seemed a bit unnecessary to me as writing a check and mailing it takes only a few minutes. Then, the two weeks stretched out to more weeks, months. Every time I called on the phone for my money, I was given a new excuse, some of them rather absurd. I finally got my money back when I threatened to call the Attorney General's office and also a consumer protection reporter on a television station and take other drastic measures. Such a process might be very hard or wearying to an older person, especially someone not in good health. So it is important to be careful, maybe even paranoid, before trusting. I was frankly shocked that the corporation involved was so irresponsible. Perhaps they spent so much money on marketing they were having cash flow problems.

Many people have been burnt worse. They have put money into promised lifetime care only to find that non-profit as well as profit making operations are underfinanced and get into financial trouble. I do not mean to malign good, reliable operations, but make sure you are doing business with one that is, not the other kind. If you pay a large sum for a unit with the promise that 90 percent or some other amount will go to your estate or be returned if you move, you want to make sure this will really happen and happen promptly.

Also, be careful to see just what daily life is like in the environment. We are all different and what pleases some people may not please others.

I was interested in one place because it advertised a swimming pool. When I checked carefully, I found out the tiny pool was only open two hours a week, one of them Sunday when grandchildren used it. Because the town required lifeguarding, the management did not spend the money for more than these two hours. I like to swim daily, but would not have been able to swim with lots of grandchildren in the small pool, and one other hour a week would have been inadequate.

Another place I discovered had a dining room that was so noisy at night that a person who likes quiet would have been miserable. Another place which offers three meals a day assigns you to a particular time to eat and you must always eat at that time. You must eat at the same table with the same assigned tablemates. Some people must eat dinner at 4:30pm – the first shift of three, the same people all the time. I would not. In fact, this place has not enough space to let you eat alone if you are tired and just want a quiet meal. Find out if trays will be brought to your unit if you are unwell sometimes.

It is very important to check out details. The former manager of one housing place told me that some units are very noisy. Check this out and also distances to shared facilities in the building. If you have a car, will your parking space be convenient and will the snow be removed from and around your car?

If the place includes a nursing home, how good is the nursing home? Visit, talk to patients, staff, and those who have relatives there and ask sharp questions.

One man who became a patient in a nursing home in a continuing care retirement community reported that there was so little staff there that when he rang the bell repeatedly for help nobody came. His wife had to stay in his room the entire time to take care of him. If you have paid in a large entrance fee to be assured of nursing home care if you need it, you don't want to have an experience like this couple had.

Certainly there are people who are very satisfied with all aspects of the retirement living institution they have chosen. They love the freedom from responsibility and the availability of new friends, facilities, and activities. They say it is the best move they have made. To be one of those, though, choose carefully and know yourself as well as your likes and dislikes and the soundness and fit of the place.

If you can afford it, there are people who, for a fee, will assist you in choosing. Make sure the one you hire is reliable and working in your best interest and not out of self-interest or profit from the place.

Best wishes in your search for a good living situation or aging in place.

Friends

It is good to have a choice of friends in your life. Not all your friends can be close intimates to whom you can pour out your heart or on whom you can utterly depend. Especially after we retire, we need variety in our lives. To depend on just one good friend is dangerous because the friend may move out, migrate, or we may have a falling out. Mental health is enhanced by having a special person in whom to confide, but we also need others with whom to do things. Some people have, for example, bridge friends or scrabble or poker friends. Some people have friends with whom they walk, shop, or go to the movies or take trips. The more friends you have, the less at risk you are for loneliness or boredom. Also, the more people you have who will be available to help should you have an illness.

As we age, we constantly have to be on the lookout for new friends. In *Be An Outrageous Older Woman*, I made a long list of new ways to make friends, and there are many more ways. Frankly, when some of my friends took to migrating for the winter, I missed them badly and had to work at making new friends. Women who are widowed also have to work at making new friends among other women alone. Often, still married friends do not include the widows in coupled events, as many widows have reported. Also, older people who get divorced or move have to work at making new friends. It is worth the effort.

I recently was very saddened by the story of a woman in one of my living alone outrageously workshops. She said she was so lonely that she had begged and even offered to bribe an adult daughter to come and live with her. It was not that this woman needed physical care from her daughter, but rather that her life was empty in retirement. What this woman needed to do, instead of clinging to the resentful daughter, was to join organizations and go to events where she could meet and cultivate people available for companionship and shared activities. Then the daughter would like her a lot better because the mother would not be so needy and would have an interesting life and be a good model for dealing with aging.

Town senior centers are a place to meet others. Library bulletin boards and local newspapers have lots of listings of organizations and events that welcome the participation of newcomers. In fact, that is how many of the snowbirds get integrated into their winter communities. Good weather is not enough as people need other people.

We are the first generation to be spending so many years as elders and as elders in retirement. We have to adapt to a new situation. The baby boomers who are coming along in the aging network can learn from us as we fill our lives well. There are so many older people around now that none of us really need to be alone unless we want to be.

Good Accumulating

Here are suggestions for some things you can accumulate without adding to the clutter in your home.

- Accumulate the names of birds and flowers by consulting a bird book or flower book.
- Accumulate new words by looking up unfamiliar words in your dictionary. We can all benefit from adding color to our vocabulary.
- Accumulate a new language by signing up for a language class at a local college which offers free or cheap courses to seasoned citizens.
- Accumulate closet space by throwing out or giving to charity clothes you will never really wear again but hold onto because you might lose weight, gain weight, change your preferences for clothes or encounter changes in styles.
- Accumulate some new friends by being friendly to people you encounter.
- Accumulate some new memories by going to new places.
- Accumulate some new recipes so you will vary your diet.
- Accumulate some knowledge by watching the courses given on Public Broadcasting Service channels.
- Accumulate some sense of priority by making

lists of things you want to do now that you are older and things you do not want to do anymore. Then work on putting into practice your lists.

- Accumulate some new dreams if you can't fulfill your old ones or your old ones are outmoded, unrealistic, or lost.
- Accumulate a wish list and let your friends and relatives know so they will stop giving you things you don't need nor want and will give you things you really do need or want.
- Accumulate a few funny stories to tell folks.
- Accumulate gratitude by writing letters of thanks, love, and appreciation to folks who have enriched your life.
- Accumulate an attitude of enjoying each day and letting go of sorrow and worry.

Ten Areas
Where We Can Choose

1. We can choose to accept our aging, despite the ageism in society and the ageism we have internalized.
2. We can choose to acknowledge our rage and express it constructively, because mad turned inward is sad.
3. We can caretake ourselves.
4. We can choose to grieve our losses, then make new connections and develop new units of "belongingness". We can help ourselves feel needed by volunteering to help others.
5. We can develop new selves when necessary and appropriate by going through an eight stage process, as follows:

- involuntary loss, or voluntary rejection of old identity
- mourning the old identity
- seeking models or mentors for change
- develop and implement strategies for change
- seek confirmation of our new identity by ourselves and others
- resist returning to the old identity
- gain increased comfort and even joy in the new identity

- repeat this process as new contingencies arise

6. We can choose good helpers in our doctors and other professionals, and we can choose to help society by being politically active
7. We can express our sexuality.
8. We can be creative in the arts and in the way we live our lives.
9. We can have recreation, and re-create ourselves by attention to our spirituality.
10. We can come to terms with frailty, disability, and our mortality.

Of course, there are some areas in which we cannot choose, and our choices may be limited in the ten areas above. Our financial situation may be limiting. Our spirit, however, expands with our years.

A Variety of Suggestions
for Older People

- Listen more than you talk. You have two ears and one mouth. Sometimes older people, especially those who live alone, tell people more than they want to hear.
- Refrain from giving people details of your illnesses, operations, aches, and pains. After 65, most people have about five chronic complaints but people prefer not to hear them.
- Since your hearing may not be as sharp as it once was, you may need a hearing aid and should not be embarrassed to use one.
- If your hearing is fading, you may talk louder than necessary and people may not enjoy this. Talking loudly is a response to the fact that we don't hear ourselves so well. So ask a good friend or relatives if you are talking too loudly.
- Do not tip the way you used to but remember you need to leave 15% for the serving person, or in cases of extra service, 20%.
- Check all your clothes for spots after you wear them. Sponge them off. As we get older we may drip more on our clothes, and our eyesight is not so keen so we may not notice spots. But others do. So hold your clothes up to a good light and check them out. We don't want to be

considered messy.

- Write down what you want to ask the doctor on your visits and write down what he or she tells you. It is easy to forget. Bring a friend or relative to take notes if necessary.
- Be good to yourself. If not now, when? Give yourself treats. Don't save everything for your heirs.
- Try to make a new friend or some new friends. You can never have too many.
- Get exercise on a daily basis. Make it a priority. You will age better if you do.
- Watch your nutrition. You deserve good food and well-balanced meals which do not have to be expensive if you use rice, beans, tofu and other non-meat foods. You can check with your local Council on Aging and Health Department to get free pamphlets and recipes.
- If you need a cane, use one. Decorate it so that it is a fun conversation piece.
- Stop economizing on electricity. We need lots of light to feel cheerful on dark days. Research shows light can help depression. Walk in a well lit mall during the winter.
- Get rid of bric a brac, electric cords, and scatter rugs on which you could trip and fall. A broken hip or limb is awful. We need to elderproof our houses the way we childproofed them when our children were toddlers.
- If you have some good stories or jokes, try to

find new people to tell them to instead of repeating them to the same people. I asked a friend to tell me if I repeated the same story to her and she said, "What makes you think I will remember?"

Possible Activities
for Older People

- Keep a journal. Start a journal writing/sharing group.
- Write poems, short stories, letters to friends, relatives, lonely people.
- Write some letters to the editor of your local newspaper.
- Cook something you never cooked before. Eat new foods.
- Go someplace you never went before. Call someone you never called.
- Make a new friend. Call up someone and invite them to tea or coffee.
- Make your own birthday cards and scrapbooks for children.
- Draw or paint on clothing for fun (make t-shirts with slogans).
- Throw things away. Get rid of clutter in your house. Simplify. Live lightly.
- Become a pen pal or a telephone pal. Help someone worse off than you.
- Arrange a potluck supper or lunch. Share your hobby.
- Go to different houses of worship.
- Read the kinds of books you have never read before.
- Have a library hour or two every day.
- Take a course. Go to an Elderhostel or conference.
- Take up birding. Get a bird book. Put out seeds for the birds.
- Get a pet or offer to pet sit for others so they can get away.
- Volunteer or get part time work. Teach something you know.
- Start a small business or give advice to someone who might.
- Change the style of dressing or wearing your hair.
- Babysit or do other chores for young families.
- Eat by candlelight and with your best dishes. Indulge yourself.
- Do a family geneology. Write a family history and your own life story.
- Read to children or do other activities with children. Offer to help in public schools or your religious school.
- Make jewelry out of old buttons or any old treasures you have.
- Make yourself go to one community event a week or more if possible.
- Rearrange your living quarters. Redecorate. Put up posters.
- Exercise to music or dance to it even when alone.
- Grow plants and talk to them.

About the author

She's Dr. Ruth
come to tell the truth

She hangs her hat
at various places that
include for example
(this is only a sample)
at Wellesley College she uses pen
at Wellesley Centers for Women.
She also teaches in Manchester, NH
at School of Human Service place
branch of Springfield College
where weekend students get knowledge.

If you want to contact her,
don't hesitate or defer.
Her address: 75 High Ledge Ave.
Wellesley, MA 02482-0142.
Phone 781-237-1793.

Other books by Ruth Harriet Jacobs, Ph.D.
  Be an Outrageous Older Woman
  Older Women Surviving and Thriving
  Women Who Touched My Life
  We Speak for Peace
  Re-engagement in Later Life
  Out of Their Mouths
  Button, Button, Who has the Button?
  Life After Youth

Another Great Book —
Seniors In Love:
A Second Chance for Single, Widowed & Divorced Seniors by Robert Wolley,
acclaimed author and counselor —and a senior himself.

6¼ x 4½", red white and gold

Show the World that Love Knows No Age!
Also order the Car Magnet
An Ideal Wedding & Anniversary Gift!

Order directly from the publisher at
www.geroproducts.com
or use the order form below (may be photocopied)

Name:			
Address:			
City/State/ZIP:			
Daytime Phone:		Evening Phone:	

QTY	ITEM		PRICE	TOTAL
	Seniors In Love Book		19.95	
	Seniors In Love Car Magnet		11.95	
			Subtotal	
Missouri residents only: at 5.25% sales tax				
SHIPPING & HANDLING: 1 item $4.95 Each additional item: $1.00 For larger orders (over $500) email for shipping price quotation: editor@geroproducts. com				
TOTAL DUE:				

Send Check or Money Order
HATALA GEROPRODUCTS
P.O. BOX 42
GREENTOP, MO 63546

Did you enjoy ABCs for Seniors?

Need more copies for friends and relatives?

Of course you do!

Golf is a good walk spoiled.
—Mark Twain

Also Available: Gift Mugs

Ideal Birthday & Anniversary Gifts!

White coffee mug with choice
of two illustrations from the book.
printed in black on two sides

Grow old
along with me!
the best
is yet to be.
—Robert Browning

Order directly from the publisher at

www.geroproducts.com

or use the order form below (may be photocopied)

Name:				
Address:				
City/State/ZIP:				
Daytime Phone:		Evening Phone:		

QTY	ITEM		PRICE	TOTAL
	ABCs for Seniors Book		19.95	
	Golfer's Mug		10.00	
	Grow Old With Me Mug		10.00	
			Subtotal	
Missouri residents only: at 5.25% sales tax				
SHIPPING & HANDLING: 1 item $4.95 Each additional item: $1.00 For larger orders (over $500) email for shipping price quotation: editor@geroproducts. com				
TOTAL DUE:				

Send Check or Money Order
HATALA GEROPRODUCTS
P.O. BOX 42
GREENTOP, MO 63546

CPSIA information can be obtained
at www.ICGtesting.com
Printed in the USA
LVOW11s1732230418

574527LV00001B/362/P